# Mission To Vienna

## *Acknowledgments*

*Many thanks to the following people for their generosity of time and cooperation: Jane Hodgman and family, Barbara Burns, Elizabeth Daniels, George Daniels III, Mary May and the entire Gourley family, Harlene Grossman, Margaret Keane, Scott Messersmith, John LeClair, Terry Sparks and Mark Taxel.*

*Special thanks to, James Gourley and Momchilo Cvijanovic. Without their eyewitness accounts, this book would not have been possible. Thank you for the countless hours of interviews, hospitality and friendship. I salute you both!*

*And finally, much love and thanks to my wife Lynn and daughters Rachel and Jessica for their love, support and patience.*

## Intro

Western Union Telegram. Date: Feb 5, 1945.

TO MRS. MADELINE GROSSMAN, BRONX, NEW YORK.

THE SECRETARY OF WAR DESIRES ME TO EXPRESS HIS DEEP REGRET THAT YOUR HUSBAND FIRST LT. ROBERT M. GROSSMAN HAS BEEN REPORTED MISSING IN ACTION SINCE TWENTY- ONE JANUARY OVER YUGOSLAVIA. IF FURTHER DETAILS OR OTHER INFORMATION ARE RECEIVED YOU WILL BE PROMPTLY NOTIFIED= STOP.

-JAMES. A. ULIO- THE ADJUTANT GENERAL OF THE U. S. ARMY

## *Chapter 1*

The weather over southern Italy in January 1945 had been mostly rainy, cold and windy, leaving behind a soaked, muddy terrain throughout the region. The U.S. Army Air Force (USAAF) heavy (H) bomber crews which included the 483rd Bomb Group were anxiously hoping to survive long enough to complete their tours of combat bombing missions against the Third Reich and return to their loved ones back home in the States. The 483rd BG was one of several heavy bomber groups joined as part of the 15th Air Force based in allied liberated territory in Italy. Between April 12th, 1944 and April 26th, 1945 the 483rd BG had racked up 5,623 missions, dropping 13,700 tons of bombs over Nazi-held territories throughout Europe during the Second World War. Taking off in Boeing B-17 "Flying Fortress's" from their base at Sterparone near the Italian town of Foggia, these brave airmen were flying strategic combat bombing missions over heavily defended targets in Germany, Austria, Czechoslovakia, Romania, Yugoslavia, Poland, Hungary, and France. The Allied armies had forced the Germans out of southern Italy and occupied existing Italian airfields and built more airbases to accommodate the many more USAAF bomb groups joining the 15th Air Force in the area in early 1944. Along with B-17's, some other heavy(H) bomb groups were flying the B-24 "Liberator" bomber. The American air crews were flying in broad daylight raids while British bomber groups were flying combat missions during the night. These bombing missions kept up for several months despite suffering heavy losses in their effort to stop the Nazi's ability to advance throughout Western Europe during World War II. Casualties among the allied airmen were high. For example, of the original air crews sent to Italy to join the 483rd bomb group in 1944, nearly forty percent were either killed, wounded, became prisoners of war, or were missing in action. They targeted oil refineries, ball bearing plants, aircraft factories, marshaling yards, shipping docks and many other manufacturing plants under Nazi control.

The 483rd bomb group consisted of four bomber squadrons. The squadrons in the group were designated as the 815th, 816th, 817th and the 840th. Unlike the American airmen stationed in England, life for the air crews based at Sterparone was a bit more primitive. Bomber crews were quartered in small tent huts. Some crews would pay the local Italians a U.S. dollar to lay down some brick for floors and occasionally for walls if there were enough brick. Each hut had a gas stove for heat placed in the middle of a few cots that served as beds for the men. There was a shower hut that only had cold water. But at least it was a shower. There of course was a latrine and a mess tent for each of the four squadrons at Sterparone. One particular member of the 483rd, a co-pilot in the 840th squadron, went as far as "borrowing" a few pieces of plumbing pipe and tapped into a water tank that was located near his and his fellow officer's tent. He then rigged the pipe to come through a hole in his hut and attached an on/off valve spout, though one could hardly call it a shower since the water came out in a single stream, much like a garden hose. Still, they were the only crew with a hut that had their own running water.

The men passed the time between flying by relaxing, playing cards or reading magazines and letters from home. If the weather were pleasant, some crews would get together with other crews for a game of baseball. For officers, a trip to the officers club was frequented spot, while the enlisted men joined their fellow squadron mates at the PX tent for a beer. Many of the young men, most in their early twenties were away from home for the first time in their lives. When off duty many of the men ventured off the base on occasion and head to the nearby town of Foggia. There they would blow off steam at the town pub and to mingle with the local Italian girls, to get away from the war for a spell. They enjoyed living it up when they could because they knew the next mission flown could be their last day on earth. While facing death was a stark reality during missions, it was rarely if ever mentioned while off duty. When not flying, the men were preoccupied with life, not death, at least on the surface of their minds.

Most of the crews of the 483rd BG had arrived in the spring and summer of 1944 with replacement crews being assigned well into 1945. For January of 1945, the 483rd and other bomber groups stationed in southern Italy had more missions scrubbed than completed this month due to the bad weather. For some perspective, the 483rd bomb group flew thirty-two missions between November 1st and December 29th, 1944. However, from the first through the twentieth of January 1945, the group had only completed five missions. But on a Sunday morning the 21st of January, the skies cleared just as the weather forecast predicted, and the mission to Vienna, Austria was finally a go!

The target for this day was The Lobau Oil Refinery. Situated a few miles south-east of Vienna along the northern edge Danube River, this oil refinery was one of a few refineries still under Nazi control. Next to importing oil from Germany's fascist ally Romania, Austria was the Third Reich's top producer of crude oil. Annexed to Germany in 1938, Austria since then had been refining crude oil for Hitler's war machine. Germany also became more reliant on synthetic oil to produce fuel. Derived from a more plentiful source, coal, synthetic oil was first developed in Germany in 1913 and was actually in production by 1919. By 1944, the Germans had exhausted much of their crude oil reserves, and with allied bombing disrupting their crude oil imports, synthetic oil was an excellent substitute for producing fuels such as gasoline while the remaining crude oil refineries the Nazis relied on could be directed more towards the production of lubricants and rubber products. The German Wehrmacht (army) had also lost its territorial gains in Russia that they had hoped to secure, including some key oil fields like the Maikop oil field in the Caucasus region. The German's captured this oil field in the summer of 1942. But unfortunately for the Germans, the retreating Russians had disabled the refinery before it fell into the hands of the Nazis. Since the badly needed drilling equipment and men to operate the refinery was competing with military requirements, the Germans were forced to withdraw from it in January 1943 to avoid being cut off after the fall of Stalingrad. This predicament was one of the reasons Germany was forced to become more reliant on its synthetic oil. Hitler had counted on capturing and holding these crude oil producing fields, so withdrawing from the ones they captured proved a critical loss. But despite more plentiful resources for producing the synthetic oil for fuel, it was still more costly to refine than their crude oil imports. So protecting the Austrian crude oil refineries along the Danube from allied bombardment was a top priority for the Nazi regime. And at the same time, the destruction of these refineries was a top priority for the allies in its effort to destroy the Nazi's ability to wage war. But for the American bomber crews including those based in Italy, the task would be costly.

The mission to Vienna had been canceled three times already during the week and by now the American heavy bombardment group including one B-17 bomber crew, led by pilot 1st Lt. Robert (Bob) Grossman, were filled with even more anxiety than the usual jitters they experienced before a mission. For one thing, Lt. Grossman and crew, already veterans of several missions including two prior missions to Vienna, knew that the German intelligence was excellent and by now was aware of the target the Americans based in Italy intended to strike this day. And with a forecast for only partly cloudy to clearing skies over the target, the enemy would be waiting to greet them. Another cause for concern was that the vicinity around Vienna and the oil refinery had approximately four to five hundred German anti-aircraft gun emplacements. It gave the crews a sick feeling in the pit of their collective stomachs. Though most of the crews managed to do their jobs effectively, they rarely outwardly showed or even spoke of their fear. But as much as they suppressed their fear, it was a constant feeling. Like the oil fields of Ploesti, Romania, Vienna was noted as heavily defended. Though the Luftwaffe was not the juggernaut it once was earlier during the war, it still had lethal weapons like the newly developed and first operational jet propelled fighter plane designed for aerial combat. The Me 262 jet nicknamed "Sturnvogel "(Storm Bird) was much faster than the allies' fastest propeller-driven fighters such as the much heralded P-51 Mustang, which the allies used as bomber escorts to various targets. The German jets could wreak havoc on the much slower bomber formations. The first Me 262 jets went into service in mid 1944. By the war's end, this jet fighter claimed 542 allied kills. If the bombers were lucky enough to escape an ME 262 attack before reaching the target, then the anti-aircraft guns would open up and fill the sky with deadly flak, only to have at times, the German fighters reappear on the bomber formation's return trip, and prey on damaged bombers limping home. German anti-aircraft batteries were responsible for downing over 3,100 allied aircraft in 1944-1945. The anti-aircraft guns fired mostly 88mm shells and for higher altitudes, 105mm shells, which had fuses set to explode above 30,000 ft. One shell from a German 88 or 105mm anti-aircraft gun had the potential to down a B-17 if it exploded within thirty yards of the plane by sending hot shrapnel traveling at one thousand miles per hour ripping through the aircraft and at times its crew. Even at two hundred yards, a detonation of flak could inflict serious damage and injury. The American bomber crews were among those who suffered tremendous casualties caused by flak. At the height of the strategic air war, American bomber crews' life expectancy was a mere two weeks! In 1942 at the start of the US bombing campaign in Europe, pilots and crews had to complete twenty-five missions before being rotated back home to the States. Military psychological experts had advised bomber Command that twenty-five combat missions were the limit air crews could take before reaching the pinnacle of what was then termed by the Army Air Force as "combat fatigue." What is known today as post-traumatic stress disorder or PTSD. By mid-1944, as bomber crew casualties mounted, the need for fully trained air combat personnel became desperate. The Army Air Force decided to raise the mission total requirement to thirty-five missions. But soon after, they were raised again to fifty combat missions. Besides the stress of facing the enemy in the skies over Europe, the missions themselves could last from four hours to as much as eleven hours flying at 30,000 feet in freezing temperatures of fifty below zero. Crews had to wear heated flying suits to keep warm during the flight. But these suits were heavy and very cumbersome and made moving about the plane very difficult especially when attempting to bail out of a flaming bomber. The flights were usually filled with hours of uneventful boredom while flying to and from the target. But the twenty minutes over the target area was a sheer terror! As the bombers reached the initial point (IP) which began the bomb run, they had to fly straight and level to maximize the formation's accuracy of bomb hits on the target. At this point the bomber formation was at its most vulnerable and suffered the most losses to flak. The allied bombers could take no evasive action until their bombs were released. At this critical juncture of the mission, they were literally "sitting ducks." Flying heavy bombers during the bomb run usually between twenty-five and thirty-two thousand feet, the formation had to at times fly through a virtual wall of flak. Having to complete fifty combat missions before being rotated back to the States led many bomber crews to suffer the beforehand mentioned PTSD or "combat fatigue" as reported in their files. In an attempt to alleviate combat fatigue, bomber crews often were sent to rest camps after every fifteen or so missions for R&R. Most times the crews of the 483$^{rd}$ went to the island of Capri located in the Tyrrhenian Sea off the southern edge of the Gulf of Naples for rest camp. There they could relax and engage in many activities like baseball, tennis, swimming and other sports and recreation. Of course, they could also enjoy a few drinks at one of the local watering holes on the Isle. And many of the bomber crews did just that.

## *Chapter 2*

Twenty-five year old 1st Lt. Robert M. Grossman had already completed forty-six missions. He was getting so close to the magic number of fifty. He was so hoping to complete just four more missions before returning home to New York. He joined the Army Air Corp in 1943, so he could do the thing he enjoyed the most…FLY! Of course, his wish to serve his country in time of need was a major contributing factor as it was for many young men in his generation. Raised in a Jewish family in Bronx, New York, Lt. Grossman felt it a duty to join the war effort and make his contribution to stopping Hitler's genocidal madness. After completing pilot training, Lt. Grossman and his newly assembled crew had two months of intensive flight training in strategic bombing and reported to Hunter Field, Savannah, GA in early July 1944. They then received orders to fly overseas by way of the northern route to Italy, with stops at Manchester, NH, Goose Bay, Labrador, the Azores, Marrakech and Tunis. They arrived at Foggia, Italy and assigned to the 483rd bomb group, 840th squadron on August 16th, 1944. This was the crew he would fly into battle. He knew how important it was to be a good team leader and in return trust the abilities for which each crew member was trained to perform. Upon arriving at the base, Lt. Grossman met with the base commander and was then assigned a hut for him and his officers. The enlisted men were shown their quarters. They were all young men, excited and anxious to give the Nazi's hell. After settling in their quarters, a few of the enlisted crew wandered over to the end of the airfield where they came across a disabled B-17. When they crawled in to look inside the damaged bomber, it was riddled with bullet and flak holes. They peeked inside the open hatch under the nose of the B-17 and were horrified to find that it was splattered with blood and the few pieces left of an airman's remains. Their "gung ho" excitement immediately dissolved into fear!

 As an air cadet Lt. Grossman married his sweetheart Madeline. A determined young lady just shy of her eighteenth birthday, she was quite certain her brave pilot was the man she wanted to share the rest of her life with. Despite getting married during a time of war that would place her husband right in the middle of aerial combat in just a few months time, she was confident he'd return home safe.

Lt. Grossman and crew began flying combat missions on August 23, 1944. As time went on and the missions mounted, occasionally replacements would fill in for some of the regular crew members who were off on rest furlough at Capri. For the mission to Vienna on January 21st, 1945, the crew consisted of battle-hardened veterans of air combat that included bombardier 1st Lt. Thomas Keane. Just four days away from celebrating his twenty-fifth birthday, Lt. Keane hailed from Boston, MA. He had forty-four missions completed. Lt. Keane was a quiet sort but always loved a good joke. He stood at 5ft 7 inches which made him the crews shortest member. A devout Catholic, Lt. Keane had joined an Air National Guard unit soon after the Pearl Harbor attack. He then requested the Army Air Corp in the hopes of becoming a pilot. But with a long list of cadet pilots in waiting, a recruiter suggested he become a bombardier as there were more openings for such positions. So it was off to San Angelo, Texas for bombardier school. After completing his training, Lt. Keane was eventually assigned to Lt. Grossman's crew. Navigator 1st Lt. George Daniels twenty-three years old from New Rochelle, NY; thirty-six missions; nicknamed "Sandy" because of his sandy blonde hair. Engineer/top turret gunner Tech Sgt. Robert LeClair, twenty-two years old from Keene, NH; forty-five missions. Sgt. LeClair came from a low-income family with his Father and Brother already serving in the Navy. Sgt. LeClair had his pilots license in civilian life before joining the Officers Flight School after the war broke out in the hope of flying for the US Army Air Corp. He was the only pilot recruit in his class without a college education. He most was likely accepted for pilot training due to his experience as a private pilot. Unfortunately, he eventually washed out of flight school due to an altercation in which he punched a fellow recruit who had been part of a group of cadets who had constantly been harassing him for being the only man without a college background in the class. That ended Sgt. LeClair's hope of flying as a pilot in the Army Air Corp. So he transferred to gunnery school and with his knowledge of flying, became a flight engineer, and was assigned to the 483rd heavy bombardment group. Left waist gunner/armorer S Sgt. Earl Baker twenty-five years old from Baltimore, MD; forty-one missions. Sgt. Baker who stood at 6 ft 1 inch was the tallest crewman. The following crew members were filling in for the regulars who were at the rest camp on Capri. The replacements were, co-pilot 2nd Lt. Carlos Escardo from Lima, Peru; eleven missions completed. Lt. Escardo, the oldest crew member at twenty-nine years of age, had traveled to the USA in 1940 to train as a commercial pilot for Pan American Airways. He came from a prominent Peruvian family and was familiar with several languages.

After the Pearl Harbor attack, he felt it a duty to join the Army Air Corp since America had given him an opportunity to learn to fly commercial planes. Because he was from a family with affluence with certain political connections, the Army Air Force assigned him to the Pentagon. However 2nd Lt. Escardo found a way to get himself assigned to a combat crew overseas and flew on to Italy. He joined as co-pilot of the Lt. William Haskins B-17 crew who was part of the 840th squadron in the 483rd bomb group and began flying in October 1944 with the same bombing squadron as Lt. Grossman's crew. What is interesting is that Lt. Escardo listed his brother as his next of kin in his military file because he did not want his parents to worry knowing he was flying combat missions. He also listed General Armando Reveredo of the Peruvian Embassy in Washington D.C. as his person to contact in the event of an emergency. Radio operator Tech Sgt Stanley Taxel, 22 years old from Brooklyn, NY; forty-eight missions. Like the other replacements, he was filling in to bolster his nearly completed mission requirement. Sgt. Taxel had an interest in photography and besides his radioman duties, he was responsible on occasions for operating the planes reconnaissance camera located in the belly of the B-17. He brought along his own "box" camera. He had taken pictures during missions with his original crew many times before. Right waist gunner S Sgt. James Gourley, twenty-six years of age, from Lycan, CO; forty-eight missions. Sgt. Gourley, son of a wheat farmer who lived out in the country in southeast Colorado, enjoyed riding his horse and fishing, but at times found farming a tough life consisting of hard physical work from sun up until sundown. After high school, he decided to go to college.  He was attending a business college in Amarillo, Texas when he got news of the attack on Pearl Harbor. Sgt. Gourley joined the Army Air Corp a few months after in the hopes of becoming a pilot. But after attending air cadet basic and college training in Florida and Iowa and making it all the way to Santa Ana Army Air Base in California for the final phase of flight training, he was passed over along with several other trainees. But this set back wouldn't keep Sgt. Gourley on the ground as he was then offered and accepted air gunnery training and was soon sent to the Las Vegas Army Air Base in Nevada to begin air gunnery training.  Ball turret gunner S Sgt. Virgil Sparks 19 years old from Cincinnati, OH; forty-one missions, and tail gunner S Sgt. Russell White 20 years old from Longmont, CO; forty-five missions completed. So, fortunately, all the replacements had many hours of combat flying experience. Before the mission, Sgt. Baker said to Sgt. Gourley (whom he was already acquainted with since Sgt. Gourley flew as a replacement with the Grossman crew before), "Thank God we don't have any rookies!" They knew that having any crew members with little or no combat flying experience would only add to the tension of the mission. A bomber crew is all about teamwork. Any mistake by an inexperienced crew member could have deadly consequences. So it was a relief to have replacements that had flown several combat missions.

During a mission, the 483rd bomb group's four bomber squadrons consisted of three squadrons flying seven B-17 Flying Fortresses, while one squadron would fly only six planes for a total of twenty-seven bombers representing the whole bomb group. Depending on the scale of the mission, at times only three squadrons of the 483rd would be able to take to the air while one squadron would be off flight duty or so ground crews could service battle damaged aircraft. Ground crews often worked through the night to prepare their plane for the mission to come. The ground crew was an important part of the bomber group. Without the dedication to their work, the bombers could be in trouble before even reaching the rally point. They were invaluable to the air crews for keeping the bombers flying. Like the air crews, ground crews were a team, and they took their job very seriously. They felt responsible if their plane had to turn back before completing its mission. Flight crews formed an unbreakable bond with their ground crew, and it was no different for Lt. Grossman's crew and the respect that they had for their ground personnel.

After an early morning breakfast, followed by the target briefing attended by the officers Grossman, Escardo, Keane and Daniels, they joined the enlisted crew Gourley, LeClair, Taxel, Baker, Sparks, and White and assembled for the jeep ride out to their B-17 Flying Fortress #44-6423. Lieutenants Daniels and Keane managed to snag a few extra flak jackets to line the inside of the bombers nose compartment to give them a little more protection when they faced enemy fire.

The briefing was all too familiar since this crew, except co-pilot 2nd Lt. Escardo, had bombed Vienna before and therefore they were fairly aware of the target details and the potential danger to come. As the crew arrived at their parked B-17, they started getting into their heated flying suits. Lt. Grossman inspected the bombers' undercarriage then climbed aboard followed by 2nd Lt. Escardo to get ready for the pre-flight check. Lt. Escardo started out reading the pre-flight check to Lt. Grossman who acknowledged and confirmed each item on the checklist. Sgt. Baker, besides being the plane's left waist gunner was also the armorer. He was busy inspecting the plane's ammo belts and bomb load.

Lt. Keane was inspecting the optics and with a thin cloth, began polishing the lens view on his Norden bombsite located up front in the nose of the plane. Also part of his routine was to make sure the bomb site was properly functioning with the plane's autopilot. As a bombardier, Lt. Keane had to take over flight control of the bomber during the bomb run over the target. By using the hand grips of the bomb site, which connected to the plane's flight controls, he had to steer the bomber over the target. As the plane reached the initial point (IP), which was the designated navigational point to start the bomb run, Lt. Grossman would then turn over the flight control to Lt. Keane. It was a very difficult task to do while being attacked by fighters of flying through flak. It took incredible focus to guide the bomber over the target using the bomb site as a "joystick" until the bombs were released, no matter how heavy the enemy flak was. After Lt. Keane's "bombs away!" call, the pilot immediately would take back the flight controls. The formation would then turn away from the target and meet up at the rally point (RP) before heading back to their home airbase. With Lt. Keane's main job complete, he would then man the twin .50 caliber machine guns by way of a remote-controlled electric "chin turret" which was mounted just below his position in the nose of the plane. Many times German fighters would hit the bomber formations head on. Bombardiers would be dangerously exposed while they tried desperately to fend off these attacks.

Navigator Lt. Daniels joined Lt. Keane in the nose to lay out his maps and charts while the two engaged in a bit of small talk. As navigator, he wasn't too concerned about locating the ground checkpoints en route to the target because for one thing, they would be flying in the number five position of his squadrons' seven plane grouping as part of the larger formation, which meant that all they had to do was follow the lead plane to the target. Still, he went through the routine of calibrating his navigational instruments in the event the lead plane and/or others in the formation were shot down or suffered mechanical problems and would have to drop out of the bomber formation, leaving Lt. Grossman's plane in the lead of the bomb run. It was also the navigator's job to direct the pilot to friendly airfields in the event they suffered battle damage that would prevent them from making it back to their base.

Sgt. Gourley commented to his opposite waist gunner Sgt. Baker "I have a bad feeling about this particular mission. I don't think I'm coming back! In fact, when I woke up to get ready, I even told my tent-mate to pack all my belongings in my duffle bag and take them down to headquarters if I don't return." Sgt. LeClair heard what Sgt. Gourley was saying and agreed. "I have the same feeling Jim! But what the hell can we do about it now?" Sgt. Baker tried to reassure his comrades and replied, "Hey boys, it'll probably be like our last mission. Remember? It was an easy milk run…no problems." But even Sgt. Baker thought to himself that something out of the ordinary might happen on this mission. They would call this feeling "flyer's premonition." The Colonel, who was the pilot of the lead plane for this mission, came by as was typical of him to check on the crews as they were assembling near their planes. Sgt. Gourley approached him and explained his uneasy feeling and asked the Colonel if he could be relieved of this mission and perhaps fly the next one instead. "Tough Shit! You're flying today sergeant!" replied the Colonel. Without any further protest, Sgt. Gourley replied a quiet "yes sir."

Tech Sgt. Stanley Taxel was checking his radio equipment in the radio room. At first, his radio frequency check revealed that although the radio transmitter was working fine, the receiver was working intermittently. But right before take off, the radio problem seemed to resolve itself during his radio check. He then checked the plane's medical kit to make sure it had the necessary supplies in the event any crewman needed medical attention during the mission. As protocol, B-17's radio operators were also trained as the plane's first aid man. T Sgt. Taxel was making his first flight with Lt. Grossman but was quite familiar with Sgt. White as together they were part of his original crew. With an interest in photography, Tech Sgt. Taxel brought along his box camera in case he might take some photos of the mission as he had done on other missions. He knew how to speak a bit of German as did Lt. Escardo. Little did he know that his knowledge of the German language would become quite useful this day forward. Ball Turret Gunner Sgt. Virgil Sparks climbed into the plane and found a spot between the two waist gunners Gourley and Baker and tried to relax before getting airborne. He was greeted by Sgt. White who was plugging in his heated flying suit. He and Sgt. Sparks would only get into their combat positions in the tail and ball turret when the formation reached altitude or within the enemy fighters range. Until then, Sgt. Sparks was yucking it up with Sgt. White and the crew with a few jokes he had heard the night before.

Tech Sgt. LeClair  was busy going over the planes mechanics, hydraulics and oxygen tanks. At thirty thousand feet, oxygen was as important as the plane's fuel. As the ship's airborne mechanic, the B-17 was his "baby." He knew everything about the bomber and would also assist Lt. Grossman and co-pilot Lt. Escardo by checking off the plane's cockpit gauges in critical situations. He was also responsible for transferring fuel by hand pump located just behind the bomb bay, from one engine to another should the fuel capacities become threatened due to damaged fuel tanks.  Before and after the enemies range on missions, he often positioned himself just behind the pilots on the flight deck. When they arrived over enemy territory or within the range of the German fighters, he would climb up in his top turret and man his twin fifty caliber machine guns and be on guard against enemy fighter attacks. But if he was needed to help the pilots regarding in-flight mechanical problems brought on by battle damage, he was always at the ready. Many flight engineers like T Sgt. LeClair were credited with helping crippled bombers make it back to the safety of their base by their quick thinking and making good use of their mechanical inclination under extreme pressure.

With the flight checklist complete and the crew in take-off positions, the B-17 started the first of its four engines. As the engines roared to life, the massive bomber moved forward and joined its place in line with the rest of the bombers in the 840th squadron to taxi out to the runway. The other squadrons of the 483rd bomb group were also making their way to the runways to prepare for takeoff.

This mission to bomb the Lobau oil refinery would be joined by other bomb groups who were also targeting the Schwechat oil refinery located southeast of Vienna. A total of one hundred and seventy B-17's from various bomb groups were only part of the planes taking flight on this mission. Another one hundred and thirty-one P-51Mustangs and P-38 Lightings joined as escort fighters for the mission to Vienna. Flying out of several fighter bases in southern Italy they included the famed Tuskegee Airmen, the first all African-American combat fighter group. Known by B-17 crews as the "Red Tails" because of their planes distinctive red painted rudders, they gained an excellent reputation for protecting bomber formations from enemy fighter attack despite facing fierce aerial combat. In fact, two Tuskegee pilots would soon be lost to enemy fire on this mission, and another would be wounded as he made his way back to base.

One by one the B-17's rolled down the runway and into the air. As Lt. Grossman's bomber turn came, he told the crew using the plane's intercom, "Pilot to crew, prepare for takeoff! Escardo, make sure the cowl flaps stay open till we get in the air." "Cowl flaps open Lieutenant" replied Escardo. He pushed the throttle forward and B-17 serial #44-6423 started down the runway. Inside the plane, the noise of the four, nine cylinder R-1820 Curtiss-Wright "Cyclone" engines was deafening.

With a full bomb load, they needed every inch of the runway before the bomber would become airborne. 2nd Lt. Escardo called out the airspeed while Lt. Grossman kept his feet on the rudder pedals making slight corrections to keep the huge bomber straight down the runway. "Airspeed sixty-five….seventy-five…..one-hundred…one-ten, one-fifteen, rotate Lieutenant!" And with that, Lt. Grossman pulled back on the wheel attached to the yoke and the bomber lifted gently off the runway. Slowly the B-17 climbed and circled until they took their place in the bomber formation. One squadron was off flight duty while the other three squadrons of the 483rd were assigned this mission. With all the bombers joined in formation they headed north and then out over the Adriatic Sea.

## Chapter 3

The weather was clear with a few clouds framed by blue sky over the Adriatic as a total of one hundred and seventy B-17's including the three squadrons from the 483$^{rd}$ climbed to 10,000 ft. At this time Lt. Grossman gave his crew the order to put on their oxygen masks. This was standard procedure once bombers reached 10,000 ft in altitude. They then climbed to cruising altitude of 30,000 ft to rendezvous with the fighter escorts. The bombers of the 483$^{rd}$ on this mission would fly in staggered groups of seven planes in tight formations known as a combat box. Each combat box consisted of a squadron of six or seven B-17's and was coded with names "Able" which was the lead combat box in the center of the formation, and "Fox" which was the squadron on the left and "Baker" which formed up the combat box to the right. Each plane's position was numbered 1, 2 3, 4, 5, 6 and 7 in each box. For example, if you were flying in the code-named "Able" combat box in the lead plane in the center of your bomber group's formation, your call name would be "Able One" or simply "Able leader." In each combat box, three planes formed a half diamond (or triangle) with the number one plane flying the point while numbers two and three planes flying behind number one to the right and left respectively and staggered. Then three more planes numbered four, five and six would form the other half of the diamond also staggered and slightly behind B-17 numbers 2 and 3 with the odd number 7 plane flying the rear of the combat box behind the number 6 bomber. This plane was known as "Tail end Charlie" and usually was flown by the least experienced crew but was vulnerable to fighter attack due to having its flanks exposed. This position was referred also referred to as "coffin corner." This type of formation was flown to maximize their firepower against enemy fighters, and offensively it concentrated the release of bombs on a target. The lead plane of the entire combat wing was called the "Flight Leader." The flight leader was in charge of leading the whole mission to and from the target. The pilot acting as the flight leader was usually a high ranking officer such as a Colonel. If the flight leader was to be shot down, then his number two would resume the lead position. Besides the danger of being under fire, avoiding mid-air collisions with other bombers in the formation was always a concern for pilots. It took amazing skill as a pilot when flying so close together during combat missions. Many crews were lost due to such mid-air collisions, even before reaching their target, especially when cloud cover limited a pilot's view.

Flying in the number five position, Lt. Grossman was flying on the right side of the rear portion of the 840th's combat box. "Thank God we're in the number five," said navigator Lt. Daniels to Lt. Keane who was hovering over his bombsite. To Lt. Daniels this meant that he could perhaps relax a bit on the way to the target since he was not the lead navigator in their combat box. He figured as long as they stayed in formation, the lead plane's navigator would be responsible for leading the group to the target. Still, he knew all navigators would have to be at the ready to take over in the event the lead plane (or planes) would pull out of the formation due to damage from enemy fire or in-flight mechanical problems leaving the next plane in line to take over as a squadron leader. Radioman Tech Sgt. Taxel called out the radio fixes to Lt. Daniels as the formation passed certain position points en route to the target. These radio fixes would come off homing beacons and even radio station towers. Sgt. Taxel would render these position reports about every thirty minutes. The position points would aid Lt. Daniels in plotting their location. With the enemy line and target still hours away, the crew settled in. T Sgt. Taxel picked up an American armed services radio station in an allied sector in southern Italy playing an old church hymn. He piped it through the plane's intercom. The hymn was "God Will Take Care of You".....which had a calming effect on the crew, especially for Sgt Gourley who had been thinking about his earlier "uncanny feeling" he had back at the base before takeoff. Cruising at 30,000 ft the sky was filled with bombers as far as the eye could see according to right waist gunner Sgt. Gourley. Left waist gunner S Sgt. Baker was complaining that his heated flying suit was not working properly. It seemed to be only generating small amounts of heat through his electrically heated suit. With the temperature dropping to minus fifty-seven degrees, S Sgt. Baker was doing his best to keep as warm as possible while he checked the hose connection coming from the electric heater. Both Sgt White and Sgt. Sparks were experiencing similar problems with their flight suits. After a struggle to find and prepare to fix the problem, inexplicably, the heat started blowing the soothing heat throughout their suits.

Sgt. Taxel picked up some weather info on the plane's radio that was passed on by "Able Leader's" radio man and informed Lt. Grossman and navigator Lt. Daniels that they would soon be facing a fairly strong headwind. Now their B-17's, with a full complement of bombs, would burn more of their precious fuel on route to the target, a concern because they weren't carrying extra gas containers for this mission. But it didn't seem to worry Lt. Daniels because he figured that after they dropped their bombs over the target, they could expect a nice tailwind to push them on the route back to the base and therefore burn less fuel. That is IF the winds don't happen to shift. All crews in the formation were hoping that they would receive that nice tailwind on the return trip to their base.

It wasn't long before they flew into the dreaded headwind. The B-17 suddenly started to bounce and shake. This headwind seemed to be stronger than the typical ones the crew had flown through during other missions. Lieutenant's Grossman and co-pilot Escardo were doing a great job of keeping the bomber's place of the box formation despite the turbulence. Lt. Grossman checked in with engineer Tech Sgt. LeClair regarding fuel consumption. He wanted him to be at the ready in case they took any flak hits in the fuel tanks and to make sure the self-sealing tanks stayed sealed and to be ready to man the fuel transfer hand pump. Lt. Grossman thought with God's help, together with an empty bomb load, a nice tailwind would allow the men to conserve just enough fuel to make it back.

Sgt. Taxel started picking up Axis Sally on the radio and piped her through to the rest of the crew. Others in the crew, such as tail gunner Sgt. White, preferred her other nickname,"Berlin Bitch." The crew never took her seriously, but they always got a kick out of listening to her sultry voice coming through their earphones, pleading for the boys, including those of the 483rd bomb group, to give up the fight. She'd always say things like "why should you nice handsome boys have to die in combat when you could be back home in the arms of your sweethearts." But most of all the crew loved the great big band music she would play between her monologues. She would at times even dedicate a song to a certain squadron's commander and tell him that "it's too bad you are flying in a war your nation is only going to lose, while your girl is at home kissing the lips of another man." Axis Sally was, in fact, an American woman named Mildred Gillars. She was born in Portland, Maine in 1900. She left the USA in 1929 for Paris where she worked as an artist's model. She returned to the US briefly before moving to Dresden, Germany in 1934 to study music. She became engaged to a German man who said he would not marry her if she returned to the States. So she agreed to stay in Germany. In 1940, she was hired by the German State Radio as an announcer. But as war broke out in Western Europe, she found herself in a precarious situation. Her fiance had to join the German army and was sent to the eastern front where eventually he was killed in action. So to avoid arrest or deportation, she signed a written oath of allegiance to Germany that convinced the Gestapo that she was loyal to the Nazi party. She agreed to work for the Nazi propaganda department in Berlin. She eventually landed the job for which she would become infamous - Axis Sally. Shortly after the war in Europe ended, she was arrested by US occupation forces and charged with treason. She was convicted in 1949 and served twelve years in a prison in West Virginia. While in prison, she converted to Catholicism. After her release, she moved to a convent in Ohio where she taught German, French, and music. She died in Columbus, Ohio in 1988 at the age of eighty-seven.

Back in the waist gunner's position, Sgt. Gourley told Sgt. Baker that he thought Sally should go to Hollywood after the war and give it a shot in radio. They both had a good laugh at that notion of Axis Sally becoming a radio star in the USA. Humor was always the perfect medicine during the missions. For Sargents Gourley and Baker, it was a temporary distraction from worrying about the German fighters or anti-aircraft 88 and 105 mm cannons that awaited them.

## *Chapter 4*

As the formation maintained its course for Vienna, Lt. Daniels was passing the time reading a book, since all seemed well with "Able Leader's" navigation. However, he had yet to plot his charts for alternate allied occupied airfields in Hungary or Russia in the event of combat damage which may prevent their bomber from making it back to Sterparone. Suddenly Lt. Keane, peering out of the B-17's plexiglass nose, informed Lt. Grossman that the Yugoslavian coast was in sight. "Pilot to Crew," Lt. Grossman called. "We are approaching the coastline. Check your guns. Make sure nothing is frozen, keep your eyes open and call out enemy fighters." Even though much of German Army had been in the south in Yugoslavia, the Luftwaffe (German Air Force) even with its depleted force, would on occasion deploy a few of the dreaded ME 262 jet fighters to intercept allied bomber formations in the form of hit and run attacks near the northern coast of Yugoslavia and around the Austrian–Hungary border. Despite a large number of allied fighter escorts, the German jets tactic would be to attack head-on and at the rear of bomber formations to take out the leader of the formation, if possible, and the lesser protected "Tail end Charlie" from the rear. Still, the sight of several squadrons of P-51 Mustang fighter planes gave the crew a sense of invulnerability, however brief the feeling would be, because as soon as the fighters reached their maximum range, they would have to turn back for home. That's when the bomber formation would be on its own to the target. Sgt. LeClair dropped down from his top turret momentarily to check the fuel consumption. He noticed the sound of the plane's engines were louder in pitch than usual. He checked in with the pilots on the flight deck. "Lieutenant?" he said. "The engines seem to be running rough. How's our fuel sir?" Down to about 10,000 pounds Sgt.." Replied Lt. Grossman. "We are burning at a higher rate than normal. This damn headwind is causing me to push these engines hard! I'm doing my best to keep our position in the formation. I think we'll be okay once we drop our bomb load. But, we better hope we get a nice tailwind on our way back." "Yes, sir Lieutenant" responded Sgt. LeClair. About this time, Able One Leader sent a message to the entire formation informing all squadrons that they were now over enemy territory. Lt. Grossman gave the crew the order, "Pilot to crew - man your stations." With that order, Sgt. White crawled back to take his gun position in the tail. Sgt. LeClair climbed up into his top turret and began rotating three hundred and sixty degrees to scan the skies above, while Sgt. Sparks climbed down into the ball turret located in the belly of the plane and did the same scanning below. Waist gunners Sargents Baker and Gourley stood at their gun position looking for any sight of fighters and observing out at the rest of the formation. Lt. Keane activated the switch that controlled the bombers twin 50. caliber machine guns mounted in the chin just below his bombardier chair. Lt. Daniels who was seated behind Lt. Keane, had been reading, quickly put down his book and secured his navigational equipment and prepared his single .50 caliber machine gun poking out through the port view window in the nose. Sgt. Taxel was at his radio desk in the center of the plane in case messages needed to be relayed to Lt. Grossman from the formation's leader.

Meanwhile, Lieutenant's Grossman and Escardo were maintaining their #5 position aka "Able 5." "Enemy fighter, nine o'clock!" called Sgt White from his tail gun position. Lt. Grossman then got on the intercom and ordered, "Pilot to the crew, be ready for enemy fighter attacks! Keep an eye on our escorts! Hold your fire until friendlies break off the pursuit. Make sure those "bogies" comes within range before firing. DO NOT waste your ammo." "P-51's are chasing Lieutenant," said Sgt White from his tail position." Suddenly another enemy fighter, a Me 262 jet appeared. "Bogie, six o'clock and closing !!" Sgt White called out with excitement. Sgt. White fired a short burst from his twin .50 caliber machine guns but hit nothing but air. The nervous tension among the crew mounted considerably at the sound of Sgt. White's twin fifty caliber machine guns firing from the rear. "You hit anything White?" asked Sgt. Gourley from his waist gun position. "No, nothing. He wasn't close enough," said Sgt. White. Lt. Grossman's voice broke in, "I thought I gave the order to hold your fire until the enemy is within range." "Sorry Lt, I thought he was heading right at us" replied Sgt White. It turns out the enemy jet was targeting another B-17 in another group of the formation. However, that particular B-17 wasn't so lucky as it took several hits and dropped out of the formation. The bomber eventually was reported as shot down with no parachutes seen escaping the stricken bomber. A few American P-51 "Mustang" fighters gave chase to the much faster German jets to no avail. Fortunately for the bomber formation, the jets broke off the attack after only a few passes, most likely due to lack of fuel, since rapid fuel consumption was a major weakness of the newly developed enemy jets. Most of these jet fighter attacks were of the "hit and run" variety.

Despite the fighter attacks ceasing, the crew was still on edge because they knew as soon as the enemy fighters broke off the attack, the German anti-aircraft guns would be opening fire on the formation as they neared their target. By this point in the war, Hitler's armies were stretched to the limit. So the German anti-aircraft gun crews were comprised of mostly teenage boys between the ages of fourteen and eighteen. These boys belonged to the Hitler Youth and were extremely dedicated to downing as many allied bombers as possible. However, most of them were hastily trained. Their lack of leadership skill caused many problems in coordinating their fire between the several gun crews. Still, at times they could be deadly accurate, even if a little disorganized. Some of these teenage gun crews would treat their job as sort of a "game" of war and showed little fear in carrying out their duty. But for the anti-aircraft crews positioned closer to the target, it was not a game at all. In fact, there were times that entire gun crews were killed by taking an inadvertent direct bomb hit during an allied bombing raid.

Escaping the brief fighter attack unscathed, the bomber formation continued on its course for Vienna. Sgt. Taxel received a weather update on his radio. The skies had been mostly clear on route to the target. "Lieutenant, I just picked up a message to the group formation. The weather over the target has broken cloud cover at approximately ten thousand feet." "Dammit, that's all we need." "Pilot to Bombardier." "Go ahead Lieutenant" answered Lt. Keane. "It looks like the target may be obscured according to weather reports of cloud cover, ten thousand feet." "Roger that" replied Lt. Keane. Just then, bursts of flak appeared and the plane shook violently as a burst came close. "Pilot to crew, check in. Any damage?" The crew all checked in with no apparent damage to report. Sgt. Sparks in the ball turret reported that the burst went off right below him, but the shards of molten metal miraculously missed them. "Pilot to navigator….how much further to the I.P.(initial point) Sandy?" "About five minutes Lieutenant," answered Lt. Daniels. The initial point was the navigational point at which the bomb run would begin, and the pilot would turn the control of the plane over to the bombardier. The flak from the German 88 and 105mm cannons started getting more intense. The black clouds of cannon bursts appeared more and more steady as the formation reached the IP. "Navigator to pilot. One minute to IP." "Roger that." "Pilot to bombardier. Be ready to take control of the ship Tom." "Roger Lieutenant" replied Lt. Keane. "Thirty seconds…..ten seconds……OK Tom….she's all yours" said Lt. Grossman as he switched to auto-pilot and let go of the yoke. "Roger Lieutenant, Bombardier has control" responded Lt. Keane. The bomb run portion of the mission was known to bomber crews as "flak alley" because it was during the time the flak guns were the heaviest..and more accurate, even at 29,500 feet. Lt. Keane had flown the bomber all the way through the bomb run. Not being able to take any evasive action, he had to hold his position the fifteen to twenty more miles to the target. As long as no one in their box group was forced out of the formation, Lt. Keane had to maintain altitude in the # 5 position of his group. The flak guns were now really opening up. The B-17 was shaking and rattling through the flak burst which was exploding in thick black and orange puffs. The crew was helpless at this part of the mission. Only by the grace of God could they be spared a direct hit which with a full bomb load, would kill them all instantly. Lt. Daniels called out, "Navigator to pilot, one minute to target." Just then Sgt. Taxel received a message from "flight leader" the lead plane of the formation. "Radioman to pilot" called Sgt. Taxel. "Flight leader reports that his bombardier can't get a fix on the target because of increasing cloud cover at 5,000 feet. We have to go around and start the bomb run again sir." "Roger that," replied Lt. Grossman, who then got on the plane's intercom. "Pilot to crew - looks like the weather forecast for clear skies over the target has changed to moderate cloud cover. Flight leader has given the order to the formation to rally left and go around start the bomb run again. Hopefully, we'll get a break in the cloud cover so we can release our bomb load." "Pilot to navigator, prepare to set rally coordinates." "Roger Lieutenant," answered Lt. Daniels. The crew was now feeling even more nervous. Having to fly through the flak once during a bomb run was bad enough, but twice on the same run, was like asking to get shot down!

With the cloud cover too thick below the formation, the flight leader hoped the clouds might part just enough on the bomb runs second attempt for his bombardier to get his bombsite fixed on the target. If successful, then the rest of the formation could drop their bombs in the proper sequence, giving the mission a greater chance of direct hits on the oil refinery. The bomber formation broke from the bomb run and circled looking for breaks in the clouds. The flak subsided a bit as they temporarily left the target area. But as they again formed up to begin the bomb run, the flak started up again. The flight leader reported that there was a break in the cloud cover, so they now had a fix on the target. Lt. Keane, resuming the flight controls, was holding the # 5 position as they came closer and closer to the target. As the rest of the formation began opening their bomb bay doors, on cue, Lt.

Keane reached for the lever to open the bomb bay doors. He pulled the lever, but the bomb bay door indicator showed the doors were still closed! Lt. Keane quickly called out to Sgt. Sparks on the intercom. Sparks had the best view of the bomb bay doors from his ball turret position just behind the bomb bay. "Bombardier to ball turret gunner." "Ball turret to Bombardier, go ahead Lieutenant" answered Sgt. Sparks. "Can you confirm bomb bay doors status?" "Bomb bay doors closed Lieutenant…repeat, bomb bay doors are CLOSED!" Lt. Keane then notified Lt. Grossman, "Bombardier to pilot - I think the bomb bay doors are frozen shut!" "One minute to target." Lt. Daniels chimed in. Lt. Keane requested that the plane's flight controls be returned to Lt. Grossman and he quickly climbed up to the flight deck and ordered Tech Sgt. LeClair to help him try to open the bomb bay doors with the manual crank. But they wouldn't budge. The minus fifty-seven degrees temperature froze the bomb bay doors closed. But being so close to the bombs away call, they could not leave the formation. They had to fly in formation with a full bomb load stuck in the belly of the plane. The formation reached the target and bombers began dropping their bomb loads. Well, most of the bombers began dropping their payloads. It turns out Lt. Grossman's B-17 wasn't the only one to have frozen bomb bay doors on this cold January afternoon. Five other B-17's suffered the same problem on this mission. As soon as the other bombers in the formation box dropped their bombs, the formation turned and headed out of the target area. Sargents Gourley and Baker could only peek outside their windows to see the effects of the bombing mission as the refinery took several direct hits. Sgt. Sparks and Sgt White had even better views as they each watched as the thick black smoke rose up through the clouds. It was only a brief distraction because as soon as they were clear of the target area, the flak started up again. The formation banked left to rally for the return trip. Lt. Grossman was doing his best to hold the #5 position, but with the added weight of the full bomb load, the rest of the formation with its empty bomb bays began slowly pulling away. Lt. Grossman and crew were gradually falling out of their slot in the box formation, so he gave the engines more throttle to catch up. Lt. Grossman was able to regain the #5 position pulling up along the right side of the #4 position bomber (Able 4). The flak was getting heavier, and the crew prayed that they'd make it through another trip through "flak alley" and that they wouldn't have any enemy fighter attacks. Doing their best to avoid the flak and keep up with the rest of the formation, co-pilot Lt. Escardo was concerned that they were using up their fuel too quickly. He looked over to Lt. Grossman and said "Lieutenant, with this heavy load, we are burning up our fuel too quickly. At this rate, I'm not sure we'll have enough to make it back!"

Suddenly flak exploded about a hundred yards in front of their formation box sending hot metal shards through the air. One piece of flak struck their bomber near the #2 engine causing a small leak in the fuel line. Lt. Escardo looked out his right side window from the cockpit and noticed a fine mist exiting the rear of the #2 engine. "That last burst must have sent a piece of flak into our #2 fuel line!" "Are you sure? Can you see any damage?!" Lt. Grossman asked. "No, I don't see any flak holes, but something is leaking out of #2" replied Escardo. "OK...said Lt. Grossman, "shut off the fuel line to # 2 and feather the prop." Feathering the prop meant that the propeller blades were turned perpendicular to reduce drag. Lt. Escardo located the fuel shut off valve for the #2 engine and switched it to the closed position. This would prevent any further leaking of precious fuel. It would also keep the engine from catching fire due to the fuel spraying over hot metal. Lt. Grossman then tried the electric fuel transfer pump to allow the remaining fuel for the #2 engine to be conserved for use in the other three engines. But it didn't seem to be working. Lt. Grossman called out to his flight engineer,"LeClair, I think we have a leak in the fuel line to #2. I shut down that line. The electric transfer pump isn't working. Go back and use the emergency hand fuel transfer to pump what's left of the #2 tank into the #1 tank." O.K. Lieutenant!" answered LeClair and he quickly went back to the bomb bay and found the hand fuel transfer pump and started pumping feverishly. "What's going on Bob?" asked Sgt. Baker from his left waist gun position. "We took a hit in the # 2 fuel line, and we need the hand pump to do a fuel transfer." "You need some help?" right waist gunner Sgt. Gourley asked. "Yeah, when I get tired pumping this fuel, you can take over" said Sgt. LeClair. "For now, keep an eye out for hun fighters - IF we can break out of this damn flak soon." The flak from the 105mm cannons was getting more accurate as Able #4 took a hit causing an engine loss and had to fall out of the formation. From the rear of Able box formation, Able #6 from the rear pulled up and into the Able 4's position.

Finally, they made it through flak alley and fortunately in one piece, but other B-17's beside Able 4 weren't so lucky. One plane believed to be from the 99th bomb group was lost to the enemy fire, last seen going down in flames. And another 483rd bomb group B-17 from the 816th squadron flown by Lt. Walter Cunningham was hit by flak and started to fall out of the formation. The entire crew eventually were forced to bail out over the Hungarian-Yugoslavian border and fortunately were picked up by Partisans and returned to Italy a relatively short time later.

With the #2 engine lost, Lt. Grossman couldn't keep up with the formation and his plane started falling behind. He soon realized that he might have to find a landing strip in friendly territory most likely in Hungary where the Russians were advancing or worse yet be forced to bail out. Flying on three healthy engines, they found themselves lagging behind by two thousand yards as the rest of the formation with empty bomb bays flew on ahead. The clear blue skies they took off into earlier that morning now gave way to heavy overcast. Lt. Keane, still perched near his bombsite, could only watch through the large plexiglas dome as the overcast skies swallowed up his view of the disappearing bomber formation. Lt. Keane realizing the bomb load was still live, called out to Sgt. Baker who was also the planes armorer. "Bombardier to left waist gunner…Baker?" "Go ahead Lieutenant" answered the Sergeant. "You better safety the fuses on the bombs. Don't want a piece of flak hitting any live bombs in the bay." "Roger Lieutenant, I'll take care of it right away." replied Sgt. Baker as he tight-roped over the six-inch wide catwalk directly above the bomb bay doors and began replacing the fuse pins on each bomb.

Lt. Grossman then got on the plane's intercom. "Pilot to crew - we won't be able to catch up and regain our position with the formation with this heavy bomb load stuck in our belly. I'll take us as far as our fuel will allow." The heavy bomber labored along the hazy sky. Each crew member by now was having thoughts of possibly having to bail out at some point. Everyone was on edge.

Lt. Daniels got on the intercom. "Navigator to pilot, I need flight leader's position to help me get a fix on our location." "OK, Sandy" replied Lt. Grossman. "I'll try to make contact with the flight leader and get an exact fix on our position." The flight leader was the lead plane in the whole formation and used its on board radar to fix positions. It was known as the radar ship for this mission. The flight leader/radar ship would call out a change in heading to the rest of the formation and straggler plane's navigators. This would be very important because they all could then get a radar fix on each of their present locations and to know when to change course.   Lt. Grossman called out to his radioman Sgt. Taxel. "Pilot to radio operator,… contact the navigator of flight leader and inform him we need his exact position right now." "Right away Lieutenant!" replied Sgt. Taxel. "Able 5 to flight leader…Able 5 to flight leader, requesting an exact radar fix. Please notify us when you change heading …over." Lt. Grossman's plane, with its still-frozen bomb bay doors and carrying the full bomb load, was lagging even farther behind the now, out of view of formation. As the rest of the formation began pulling even farther away, Lt. Grossman got back on the intercom. "Pilot to radio operator - have you heard from flight leader? I need that radar fix and heading." " I've been calling them, but they aren't responding," replied Sgt. Taxel. "Well - keep trying Sgt.!" "Pilot to navigator, do you have alternate headings to friendly bases in Hungary, I think that may be our best shot." "Negative Lieutenant" responded Lt. Daniels. Lt. Grossman called back, "What do you mean negative?" "Sorry Bob, I forgot to mark the alternate emergency headings while we were en route to the target. If we can get a true heading from flight leader, I might be able to set a new course to friendly bases." Shortly after, Lt. Escardo noticed that the gauge on the oxygen level was dropping. Unbeknownst to the crew, the oxygen line was damaged by the same flak burst that damaged the fuel line to the #2 engine during the bomb run. They would eventually have to drop their altitude below ten thousand feet, but they hoped to get to a safer fly zone before dropping that low. Still carrying a full bomb load and flying on three engines, the bomber was now several miles behind the formation. As if their predicament could not get any worse, the winds had reversed, so the crew was now facing a headwind instead of the tailwind they had hoped for on the return trip home. Still getting no response from the repeated calls to the flight leader, Lt. Grossman regularly checked in with radioman Sgt. Taxel regarding any contact with the flight leader while he and Lt. Escardo managed the flight deck. The crew had no idea at first why Flight leader or any other bomber from the mission failed to answer, but it soon became apparent to Taxel that their plane's radio receiver, which had been acting troublesome right before takeoff, was not receiving! Though their calls for help may have been heard by other planes in the formation, without being able to hear their responses for changed headings they were essentially lost and on their own.

## Chapter 5

After flying several minutes with no radio contact, the radio receiver finally sprang to life with a crackle as Lt. Grossman received a radio call from another plane. "Able 5 this is Baker 1, how can I help?" What a relief it was to finally receive an answer to their several calls. But it wasn't the flight leader. It turns out it was Lt. Grossman's original co-pilot Lt. Jack Malkemes who had become a first pilot with his own crew a month earlier. Flying in the code name "Baker" box of the formation ,Lt. Malkemes radioman heard the calls going out to the flight leader. Lt. Grossman responded, "Able five to Baker one, ..this is B-17 6423. We lost an engine and are getting low on fuel and we are down to about 50 pounds of oxygen. Request coordinates when you change heading… over," "Roger that Able five" responded Lt. Malkemes. Unfortunately, that was the last Lt. Grossman and crew would hear from anyone in the bomber formation. The radio receiver again stopped receiving. Sgt. Taxel tried desperately to get the receiver to work, but wasn't having much luck. Receiving no more replies to their many calls for a fix and heading changes, Lt. Grossman checked in again with Lt. Daniels to see if he could try to figure out their position despite the now thick cloud cover below. He ordered Sgt. Taxel to keep trying to make contact with anyone from the formation that was by now entering a safe fly space on their way back to their base. Lt. Grossman figured if the formation can hear them, someone would at least know that they were still airborne. But now their transmitter failed, and no one in the formation heard from them again. It soon became apparent to Sgt. Taxel that their plane's radio was useless without the parts he needed to get it to work. He was bothered with thoughts about the radio acting up before takeoff. When it came to life during pre-flight, he figured all was well. But now it was a useless piece of junk!

Back in the midsection of the bomber, waist gunner Sgt. Baker was looking out his window from his left side gun position for possible fighters, when he turned around to find Sgt. Gourley lying flat on his back passed out! Sgt. Baker quickly came to Sgt. Gourley's aid and noticed his face was turning blue! Baker pulled off Gourley's oxygen tube and found that the tube was frozen and blocking the oxygen flow to Gourley's lungs. Sgt. Baker grabbed a nearby spare oxygen tube and in a flash, fastened it to Sgt. Gourley's mask. Hearing the commotion towards the back of the plane, Lt. Grossman got on the intercom. "Pilot to waist gunners…what's going on back there?" "Gourley passed out Lieutenant!" replied Sgt. Baker. "Oxygen tube froze, but I hooked up a spare to him. He's breathing sir, I think he's starting to coming around." "OK, keep me posted on his condition" replied Lt. Grossman. Lt. Grossman then called on the entire crew, "Pilot to crew - KEEP CHECKING YOUR OXYGEN FLOW TUBES until we lower to a safe altitude and warmer temperatures. Can't have everyone blacking out. We are low on oxygen as it is. I will have to lower our altitude at some point pretty soon." As the fresh oxygen flowed into Sgt. Gourley's lungs, he quickly came to. "What happened?" He said to Sgt. Baker. "I just saved your neck - that's what happened!" Sgt. Baker replied. "Your air tube was frozen solid!" "Really?" said Gourley. "I don't remember a thing. One minute I'm fine, the next minute I just blacked out!" "Well, remember to check your flow tube every few minutes" added Sgt. Baker. "Yeah, I guess I was too busy looking for fighters and forgot to check for ice forming in my tube. Thanks for looking out for me." "Alright, alright, how ya feeling?" said Sgt. Baker. "I feel kind of woozy, but I'll be fine." said Sgt. Gourley.

"Pilot to navigator" called Lt. Grossman….."George, if we can break through this haze, can you get an idea of our ground location?" Lt. Daniels replied "I'll do my best. Flying through this thick cloud cover and without that radar fix, I'll need to make some DR (dead reckoning) calculations and see if I can get an approximate idea of where in the hell we are! It won't be easy since our airspeed and wind direction has changed," In short, dead reckoning determines the position of the aircraft at any given time by keeping an account of the track and distance flown over the earth's surface from the point of its last known position. In this case, the crew's last known position was just before they fell behind and lost sight of the formation. Unbeknownst to the crew, this was somewhere over the border of Hungary and Yugoslavia. However as the plane was heading south, Lt. Daniels believed the plane had drifted more to the southwest which would have put them on a course heading towards Italy. Fuel and oxygen were now becoming critical and without contact from the formation, Lt. Grossman got on the intercom. "Pilot to crew, I'm afraid we may have to abandon ship. Prepare to bail out." It left a sickening feeling in the pits of the stomachs of the airmen. For one thing, since Lt. Daniels wasn't able to get an accurate fix on their location, they wouldn't know exactly where they would be bailing out over. And they would have no idea if the Germans would capture them or they would picked up by friendly forces. Or even worse, would they be bailing out over the Adriatic Sea? Just as Lt. Grossman was about to give the bailout order, Lt. Escardo suggested dropping to a lower altitude until they broke out into the clear and could see if they were over the water or land. Perhaps if they were over land, they might recognize any land features that might indicate their location. And at least they could prepare for a possible wet landing. Lt. Grossman agreed and informed the crew that he would drop down until they were out of the cloud cover.

The dilemma facing Lt. Grossman was that while he wanted to get the bomber to lower altitude and break out of the high cloud cover, he had no idea if they were over friendly or enemy territory. Exposing themselves into clear skies might lead to a German fighter attack that would doom them for sure! But this was a risk he felt he had to take. So as he lowered in altitude to below 10,000 feet, they finally broke into the clear and were relieved to see that they were over land! The question was, were they over friendly or hostile land? Lt. Daniels was sure it was northern Italy. But most of the crew believed they were over Northern Yugoslavia. For a brief moment, Lt. Daniels asked Lt. Grossman if they should try and make it to Switzerland. But this suggestion was met with doubt as not a viable option by Lt. Grossman and crew. Landing in Switzerland would mean that the crew would have to spend the duration of the war as "guests" of the Swiss since Switzerland was a neutral country. Besides, even if they were over northern Italy, they would still need more fuel to make it the Swiss border. And fuel was running out.

Lt. Grossman noticed a river below. He lined the bomber up with the river below and ordered Lt. Keane to open the now thawed bomb bay doors and drop the bombs in the river. Lt. Keane hit the switch, and the bomb bay doors opened without a problem. Looking through his bombsight Lt. Keane released the bomb load. "Bombs away!" called out Lt. Keane. The bombs fell out of the B-17's belly and because the bombs had been disarmed they splashed harmlessly into the river without exploding. The river turned out to be the Vrbas River in Yugoslavia. Lieutenant's Grossman and Escardo were now desperately looking for a place to put the plane down. As the plane was running out of fuel, Lt. Grossman brought the plane down to 1,000 ft. With the sun now setting, he was running out of daylight too. All he could see was snow covered patches of land. Lowering to 500 feet, Lt. Escardo spotted a snow covered field that appeared large enough to land their B-17.

Sgt. Gourley peaked out his port side window and saw two women walking in the knee deep snow along a fence line. He noticed the women looking up with great surprise as the large bomber passed over them.

Lt. Grossman ordered the crew to join Sgt. Taxel in the radio room and prepare for wheels-up crash landing. Lt. Escardo remained with Lt. Grossman on the flight deck since he was the co-pilot. All the other crew members quickly assembled in the radio room and assumed their crash positions. Each man sat on the floor and with knees up and forming a backrest for the next crewman to lean up against. Each man's hands were placed against the other crewman's head to prevent any violent snapping sensation when the plane hit the ground. Sgt. LeClair was the closest to the bulkhead and used one arm to brace against the radio equipment to keep any parts from becoming projectiles.

The B-17 dropped even lower in altitude flying on three engines that were now sputtering on only fumes at treetop level. They approached the open snow covered field they had spotted. Lieutenants Grossman and Escardo were doing their best to avoid coming in at too steep an angle on the approach. Just before impact Lt. Grossman eased the nose of the bomber up just a bit. Hold on!" he shouted through the intercom, seconds before the plane plunged into three feet of fresh snow. The landing wasn't as violent as the crew expected. The snow acted as a cushion, and although the plane bounced once, it continued to slide harmlessly before coming to a stop. "You ok?" Lt. Grossman asked his co-pilot. "Yes, I think so" answered Lt. Escardo. "That was a fine landing sir!" he added. Lt. Grossman responded, "Couldn't have done it without your help Escardo!" Right away Lt. Grossman called out to the rest of the crew, "Everyone check in!" One by one each crew member checked in without any serious injuries to report. For a brief moment, Lt. Grossman was quite relieved. Crash landings are difficult enough for the best pilots, but psychologically it means the world to a pilot that his skillful landing under extreme conditions did not cause death or injury to any of his crew.

Lieutenants Grossman and Escardo quickly unbuckled their parachute harness's and gathered their "escape kits." The kits consisting of a small compass, cigarettes, chocolate bars, change of socks and underwear, extra ammo clips for their .45 caliber pistols and ID papers that included a photo resembling a passport photo taken wearing civilian clothes. The photo could aid them in forging a civilian ID in the event of bailing out or crash landing behind enemy lines. They also had G.I.

boots tied to the bag. These boots would be more suitable in the event they would need to walk long distances. The pilots then headed to the rear escape hatch where they joined the rest of the crew who were already climbing out of the plane with their escape kits into the cold dusk-lit night. Once they were safely out of the damaged bomber, and they were sure it wouldn't catch fire, the slightly dazed and nervous airmen gathered around wondering where exactly they were? Lt. Daniels was sure it was Northern Italy, but the rest of the crew were under the impression that they were in Yugoslavia. Suddenly, they noticed a crowd of civilians gathering about two hundred yards off. "Hey Bob, who do you think those people are?" Lt. Daniels asked Lt. Grossman. "I have no idea" replied Lt. Grossman. "You think they're friendlies?" added Lt. Keane. Lt. Grossman replied, "I'm not sure Tom….only one way to find out." So the crew followed their pilots' lead and slowly started walking towards the civilians. The crew was lined up in a row, shoulder to shoulder walking closer and began to notice that out of the group of civilians, a few men formed a row of about six, and mirroring the American airmen, began walking shoulder to shoulder as well towards the crew. The closer they got, it was apparent that these men were informally dressed but wearing worn out looking uniforms under heavy open coats and carrying weapons. Right behind this group, the remaining group of about twenty-five armed men followed along. Almost amusing to the Americans, it was quite a sight. Not sure if the approaching group was friendly or not, Lieutenants Grossman, Escardo, Keane, and Daniels and Sargents Baker, White, Sparks, Taxel, and LeClair looked down at their holsters for their side arms while Sgt. Gourley thought to himself in somewhat frustration because he left his .45 caliber pistol back at their base. It had the look of an old western movie with the two parties slowly closing the gap between them like a gang of gunfighters! But the American aircrew quickly decided to back off any thought of a shootout with this approaching militia because they weren't acting in an aggressive manner. Besides, the closer these men approached the crew, they could see they were not only armed, but armed with automatic weapons, grenades and belts of ammunition that crisscrossed their chests. These soldiers would likely just cut them to pieces if anyone of the crew so much as reached for his gun. Lt. Grossman ordered his group to keep calm. Both groups of men met about halfway in the middle of the snow-covered field and stopped as they were facing each other about ten feet apart. The approaching men's uniform looked somewhat unfamiliar to the crew. Perhaps they were Russians or Italians, the crew thought. But at least they were sure they were not Germans! They wore a black cloth hat and as described at first sight, their attire looked worn and dirty. They had long hair and thick black beards and had the look of guerrilla fighters. One of the men began speaking in a language none of the crew could understand except one crew member. The co-pilot 2nd Lt. Escardo had extensive knowledge of several languages and recognized the language as Slavic. His vocabulary was limited in this particular language, but a few of the soldiers spoke fluent French, German and Italian most of which he did know. Together with Sgt. Taxel's knowledge of the German language, the crew could at least communicate with these motley looking soldiers. Lt. Keane turned and muttered to Lt. Daniels "I told you this wasn't Italy." The crew had a difficult time at first convincing these soldiers that they were American. Finally, one of the bearded guerrilla fighters called out to the crew. "Amerikan?" Lt. Grossman, pointing to his blue and orange wing and star shoulder patch, answered "Yes! Yes!… American!" With that, the soldiers relaxed and cracked smiles. The nervous crew all breathed a sigh of relief. These soldiers turned out to be Yugoslavian renegades known as Chetniks ,which translates in English to, "detachment of men." The Chetniks were known to have helped allied air crews evade capture and perhaps could help them return to their base in Italy. However, the crew had crashed within a few miles of the German lines and the Yugoslavian Liberation Army (known as Partisan) lines about ten miles north of the town of Banja Luca. The Partisans, led by Communist Josip Tito, were considered Europe's most effective anti-Axis movement during the Second World War. Marshal Tito was born Josip Broz in Kumrovec, Croatia in 1892. Drafted into military service during World War One, he became the youngest sergeant major in the Austro-Hungarian Army of that time. After being seriously wounded and captured by the Imperial Russians during the war, he then was sent to a work camp in the Ural Mountains. After the war ended, he returned to the newly established Kingdom of Yugoslavia where he joined the Communist Party of Yugoslavia. In 1939 he was named General Secretary of the League of Communists of Yugoslavia and went on the become leader of the Partisans movement in Yugoslavia against the Nazi and Fascist Italian occupiers during World War Two. While communist or anti-fascist Croatians under Tito's leadership were considered friendly to the Allies, the crew had to beware of the fascists Croatian known as the Ustachis. The word Ustachi is derived from a Croatian verb, "rise up." Founded in 1930, the Ustachis were made up of ethnic Croatians. They identified themselves as a nationalist organization wanting to create an independent state. The Ustachis ideology was a blend of fascism, Roman Catholicism, and Croatian nationalism. They declared that the Catholic and Muslim faiths were the religion of the Croatian people. They believed the Bosnian's Muslim faith was a religion that kept the true blood of Croats. Heavily influenced by Nazism and fascism, they promoted a corporatist economy. Hitler and primarily Mussolini's support of the Ustachi movement were based on pragmatic considerations, such as maximizing the axis powers influence in the Balkans. In fact, Hitler initially did not support the Ustachis desire for an independent Croatia. He had stressed the importance of a strong and united Yugoslavia. He and other Nazi officials wanted a stable Yugoslavia and wanted their government to be recognized officially as neutral during the war. A neutrality agreement would allow Germany to gain Yugoslavia's raw material exports without a conflict, which would deplete more of their military resources than desired. But with Yugoslavia so divided, a neutrality pact was next to impossible. Without the pact, the Nazis needed the Ustachis' cooperation in controlling any anti-fascist groups and in return agreed to recognize a portion of the country as the Independent State of Croatia. This cooperation between the Ustachis and the Nazis also resulted in many Ustachi soldiers joining up with German army (Wehrmacht), Waffen SS and SS police units in Germany and Italian held territories in the country. The Ustachis were very much anti-Serbian. They were in fact quite brutal. Many Ustachis units committed horrific acts of violence on the Serbian population. Although Reichsfuhrer and SS leader Heinrich Himmler in particular, grew aggravated with the Ustachis lack of full compliance to the Nazis agenda of extermination of the Jews, the Ustachi permitted Jews who converted to Catholicism to be recognized as "honorary Cro-ats" and thus exempt from persecution. By the end of the war, the Ustachi were responsible for the murder of hundreds of thousands of Serbs, Romani people (Gypsies) and Jews who wouldn't convert to Catholicism and were also responsible for the persecution of anti-fascists or dissident Croats and Bosniaks throughout parts of Yugoslavia.

It all started in 1941 after the Nazi and fascist Italian occupation of Yugoslavia. The Ustachis were appointed to rule a portion of Axis-occupied territories as the Independent State of Croatia. On April 10th of 1941, Hitler had accepted Mussolini's proposal to name Ante Pavelic as the Head of State of Croatia. Loyal to the Nazis and fascist Italy, they were described as both an Italian-German quasi-protectorate and as a puppet state of Nazi Germany. Ustachi atrocities committed during the war even had German military officials questioning these ethnic Croatians methods of extermination. Many Serbian men, women, and children were killed by being mutilated, beheaded, buried alive, burned alive and other methods of a grotesque nature. The Germans preferred that all allied downed air crews in occupied territory should be turned over to German units for interrogation. But falling into the hands of a Ustachi patrol who were operating on their own could mean certain death for the American aircrew.

## Chapter 6

The Chetniks were made up of Serbian loyalists to the Imperial rule of King Peter and therefore were against the formation of Independent State of Croatia, which they feared might lead to the widespread genocide of the Serbian people instead of the localized genocide taking place in Croatian held land. The Serbian Chetniks found themselves not only in conflict with the Nazi occupation and the Nazi-supporting Ustachis, but also the Yugoslavian Partisans who desired a communist rule. Though the crew was fortunate enough to be met by friendlies such as the Chetniks after their crash landing, they were by no means safe. In short, they landed smack dab in the middle of not only a World War but a Civil War as well, with all factions only a few miles apart from one another.

All American airmen of the 15th Air Force were briefed a few months earlier, that if any allied crews were forced to bail out or crash land in Yugoslavia, that it might be better to seek the Partisans for help instead of the well intentioned Chetniks. The reason being was that the Chetniks, who were led by Draza Mihailovic, no longer held territories that included the routes and pathways that could lead them to the Mihailovics headquarters and the airfield. Five months earlier the Chetniks had successfully helped the Allies extract downed airmen in secret rescue operations like Operation Halyard where over 200 American airmen were safely airlifted out of Pranjani, Yugoslavia and returned to Italy. But by January 1945 the Partisans had a better advantage to get downed allied airmen out of enemy occupied Yugoslavia and through to the Adriatic coast where they could use boats to cross over to the island of Vis and from there airlifted to Italy. The problem was that besides the Germans, the Partisans were enemies of the Chetniks. And the crew would soon learn that the Chetniks would never turn the crew over to the Partisans. The Chetnik Sargent introduced himself as "Bosko" (not his full name, but "Boskovic" was most likely his real name.) Sgt. Bosko told the crew that they crashed about ten miles south of the city of Banji Luca. Using German as a common language, Sgt. Taxel and with a bit of help from Lt. Escardo, acted as translators. Lt. Grossman asked the Chetnik Sargent if he could help them locate the Partisans. Suddenly the Serbian freedom fighter became very agitated. "Partisans, why do you ask for help from the Partisans!?" he asked. Lt. Grossman had Sgt. Taxel translate a response. "Sargent, tell him we were told that the

Partisans had open routes to friendly territories from where they could get us to the Adriatic coast." "The Partisans will never help you get out of Yugoslavia" Sgt. Bosko replied in German. "We are your best chance!" he added. " Ok, Ok, we meant no offense" replied Lt. Grossman. As Sgt. Taxel translated his words, Sgt. Bosko calmed down. Changing the subject, Lt. Grossman explained to the Chetnik contingent that he had to burn the bomber so it wouldn't fall into the hands of the Germans. But Sargent Bosko was against this because it was getting dark and a burning plane might only alert the Germans and their Ustachi friends, or the Partisans, to their whereabouts. The Chetnik Sargent spoke in German to Sgt. Taxel who again translated his words to Lt. Grossman and the rest of the crew. Sargent Bosko made a point of warning the crew of the perils of falling into the hands of the Partisans. The crew figured this was only Chetnik propaganda, but because of the deep contempt for the Partisans exhibited in Sgt. Bosko's voice, no one in the crew let on. They had no intention of upsetting the Chetniks by voicing their partiality which favored a rescue by the Partisans based on earlier briefings. For now, the crew kept a tight lip on the mere mention of the Partisans while in the company of the Chetnik soldiers.

The importance of burning the plane was twofold; besides following standard U.S. military orders, setting it ablaze would prevent the Germans from identifying the serial number and squadron markings of their plane. Throughout the war, the Nazi's would often film or photograph downed allied planes and if possible, show off the squadron markings and serial numbers taken from the plane's rudders if they were intact after crashing. They might even broadcast the identification numbers of any crashed allied plane and boast about how they shot down the allied invader, and that all of its crew had been killed. Of course, this was all speculation as far as the crew was concerned, but at this point in the war in which the axis forces were losing, the Nazi's were more and more desperate and continued using propaganda tactics as they had earlier in the war to bolster their ranks. Only now they also were using propaganda to break the morale of the allies. The last thing any American pilot and crew wanted was to have false propaganda information such as being listed as "killed in action," possibly reaching their base in Italy. They all figured if they could get back to their base soon enough, they might even avoid the dreaded "missing in action" telegram from being sent to their families back home. It usually took about two weeks before families received MIA telegrams, so they were determined to get out of Yugoslavia as soon as possible, and the

Chetniks were their best hope in light of their present situation. So they assured their new Chetnik friends that they would allow them every chance to help get them back to allied territory. Lt. Grossman insisted that they must at least destroy the bombsite. The Norden bombsite was top secret technology. But in fact the bombsite's technology was not much of a secret to the Nazi's. They sent a spy, Herman Lang to the U.S. in 1938. Lang took a job with the Norden company and was able to reconstruct the bombsite from memory to his Nazi superiors. Lang was later arrested and charged with espionage in 1941 and sent to prison for eighteen years. Still, allied air command ordered all air crews in the event of a crash landing behind enemy lines, to destroy the bombsite at all cost. Sgt. Taxel translated this to Sgt. Bosko who seemed to understand the importance of the task. Without waiting for permission from the Chetnik Sargent, Lt. Keane climbed back in the plane and crawled up to his bombsite. While Lt. Keane was in the nose of the B-17, he set off the thermite charge that every B-17 had stored on board. The extreme heat of the chemical reaction turned the bombsite into a melted lump of metal within minutes. Meanwhile, Lt. Daniels was busy using his cigarette lighter to burn all the mission's target maps and navigation charts that he had gathered up before entering the radio room preparing for the crash landing. However, he kept a tiny compass and had also written down the longitude and latitude coordinates of the crash site just in case they were able to make contact by radio to friendly forces who might be able to pass on their location to their base in Italy. Unfortunately, this was not to be the case. A couple of Chetniks climbed aboard the bomber and began removing the plane's radio. They also removed the .50 caliber machine guns. It left an uneasy feeling with the crew. "Lieutenant, are we just going to let them take our plane apart?" asked Sgt. LeClair. " I don't like it, but who's going to stop them?" replied Lt. Grossmann. "I want to burn the entire plane, but at least the bombsite, and maps are destroyed. Who knows, maybe they can fix our radio?" he added with optimism. Sgt. Bosko motioned for the airmen to follow him up the mountain quickly. Sgt. Taxel thought how ironic it was to be using his knowledge of the German language, the language of the enemy, to communicate with Sgt. Bosko. As it turned out many Chetniks could speak German since the Nazi occupation. While the Chetniks were pro-western, some in their ranks collaborated with the German and Italian forces in a collective fight against the Partisans. They viewed the Germans and Italians as the lesser evil to the Partisans. After the Italian forces collapse and the Western Allied landing in Yugoslavia became less likely, the Germans ceased disarming and imprisoning the Chetniks like they had done so in for example in Montenegro in May of 1943, and instead, they in turn, started collaborating with the Chetniks throughout the country to some degree. The Germans adopted a "live and let live" with the Chetniks. The Germans began tactical cooperation with the Chetniks to help them fight off the Partisans. But even though the Chetniks fought mutually with Germans against the Partisans, they were not known for turning in or informing on allied airmen, though the Nazis did offer a reward to them that was the equivalent of three U.S. cents for each downed allied airmen turned in. The Chetniks were incredibly loyal to their cause. The Chetniks believed that accepting a reward from the Germans would do much more harm than good. The Chetnik leaders figured as long as they continued helping downed Allied airmen to evade capture and kept them safe from harm, this would, in turn, show the western Allies by wars end, that they were indeed loyal to the West in the fight against the Nazis. It may give them more of a future bargaining chip geopolitically should they need the support of the Western Allies once the war against the Fascist ended. But with the Allies support of the Partisans, by way of supplying them with arms so they could fight the Germans in Yugoslavia, this did not sit well at all with many Chetniks. These were not the same Chetniks from Pranjani that performed so valiantly during the "Operation Halyard" evacuation of American Airmen in August 1944. The crew was being guided by Chetniks who though they were loyal to helping downed allied air crews, seemed more jaded towards the Americans. Yes, they reassured the crew that they would be safe, but the feeling among the crew was to be compliant and not to demand any special treatment. For the time being, they adopted this attitude.

Sgt. Bosko told the crew he was taking them to their headquarters which was about a mile and a half higher up the mountain trail. Nightfall was looming, and it was only a matter of time before the Germans or worse, the Ustachis who committed horrible atrocities against their enemies, could arrive. Before marching off with their Chetnik escorts, Lt. Grossman gathered his officers Daniels, Escardo, and Keane while the rest of the crew were busy changing out of their fur-lined flying boots and into their standard land military boots they had attached to their harnesses. All accept Sgt. Gourley who was feeling around his pockets on his flight suit for some candy bars he had taken along. He figured he'd change out of his flying boots once they reached the Chetnik outpost. Lt. Grossman said to his fellow officers,"When it gets dark, I'm coming back to burn up whats left of our ship." "Do you think it's necessary Bob?" asked Lt. Daniels. " I burned our charts, and

Tom took care of the bombsite. Besides this place might be crawling with Germans by then. It's like asking for trouble!" "I understand that Sandy, but we have orders to destroy the ENTIRE plane if and when possible. I think we can do this under cover of darkness" replied Lt. Grossman. "What about our, ..eh hmm, "friends?" Lt. Keane asked. " I'm sure they're going to have something to say about it if we torch the plane after telling us not to." Lt. Grossman answered,"Well Tom, we'll just have to convince them that we have orders to destroy our plane if we come down in enemy territory. Luckily, we crashed landed in territory that for now is held by these guerrilla fighters and not the Germans." "At least not yet," said Lt. Escardo. "Though I don't think the Germans will be out patrolling these mountains in this freezing weather tonight" he added. Lt. Grossman continued, "That's right Escardo. And I don't think that any civilians will be outside in the dark of night either. Lt. Grossman paused."Look, we might not get another chance to burn up the plane!" If we do get a chance, I'll take LeClair with me. He'll know how to ignite the fuel vapor if there's any left in the tanks."

Despite being advised from allied command to seek out the Partisans for help, the crew for the time believed they were in good hands with the Chetniks. Aside from a bit of apprehension, they felt they had no choice. After all, the Chetnik soldiers were behaving non-aggressively towards them, and no attempt was made to disarm those crew members that had their sidearm's holstered. And knowing he would most likely have to figure out a way to convince the Chetniks to support their need to destroy their plane, Lt. Grossman and crew were going to have to trust their new found friends.

The crew was led away by Sgt. Bosko and the contingent of Chetniks soldiers. Off they went in single file marching through the knee-deep snow, leaving behind the remains of their lifeless bomber.

After a while of trekking slowly up a snowy mountain trail, the dusk turned to night. The crew could hear gunfire in the distance. Lt. Grossman spoke up. "Sgt. Taxel, ask Bosko what all the gunfire is about." "That is the Partisans and Germans fighting," Sgt. Bosko said almost nonchalantly. "The Partisans are pushing the Germans out of the south. But they will never fight us in these mountains because we will defeat them if they (Partisans) try!" he said boldly. The crew was feeling cautiously optimistic. If the Partisans were indeed advancing from the south, then the crew believed the Germans would soon have to retreat north leaving the area they crashed landed in a safe zone, so they hoped. But it could also mean they could be picked up by the northbound retreating Germans if they tried to get to the low country where the routes to eventual freedom were located.

Eventually, the crew came upon a small two story windowless stone house that stood as a Chetnik headquarters for this sector. They were ushered in through a narrow doorway and into a dimly lit room. This small room was the Chetnik Commandant's office. A Chetnik who spoke some English greeted them. He introduced himself as Colonel Junic. Though a bit older, he resembled the same Chetnik soldiers that escorted them from the crash site. Wearing a long, dirty looking wool coat similar to ones worn by Russian soldiers, he had long hair with a beard and wore belts of ammo that crisscrossed his chest as if to indicate he had fought in several battles. But the ammo belts had no missing bullets and looked in very good condition as if they were never used in any battle. He also had a few grenades and a long-bladed knife attached to his belt line. His clothing gave no clue to his rank, but he was the man in charge of this sector of the mountain region. The crew noticed that he and the Chetnik escort soldiers were constantly scratching the back and sides of their heads. Sgt White leaned over to Sgt. Gourley and quietly asked "Why the hell are these guys itching so much?" "Beats me, maybe it's fleas!" Sgt. Gourley quipped. Sgt. White just looked down and cracked a smile. Unknown to the crew, the Chetnik soldiers had a bad case of lice! Most of the Chetnik soldiers slept on piles straw in barns, hardly ever removing their clothing, let alone bathing, in the winter. Col. Junic addressed the crew, and in broken English, he began the basic process of asking each of the Americans their name and rank. He seemed curious about the their backgrounds and what they thought about President Roosevelt. He asked each crewman where in America they hailed from. Each one answered. "New York, Cincinnati, Boston, Colorado, Brooklyn, Baltimore" and so on. "Do not worry, we WILL get you out." Col. Junic assured the crew. Lt. Grossman asked the Colonel. "How long before we return to allied territory?" "Very soon, very soon Lieutenant" he responded. "But we must protect you from the Partisans," he warned. "You cannot trust them! They will never get you out of Yugoslavia!" he added. Lt. Grossman nodded in agreement even though he didn't believe the Colonel. Thinking back to their encounter with Sgt. Bosko earlier, any talk of the Partisan's ability to better help the crew mentioned in front of the Chetniks would only hamper their effort to get back. Back at the crash site, Lt. Grossman had at first underestimated the fact that the Chetniks were not only engaged in a civil war with the Partisans, but they HATED them more than the Germans! While they fought against Nazis occupation, by 1945 many Chetniks believed that communism was more of a threat than fascism.

Col. Junic went on to explain that since they had the plane's radio removed from the plane, it could be used to contact the crew's airbase in Italy and let their American comrades know that they were, in fact, safe and uninjured. The Chetniks had taken the radio to another nearby Chetnik outpost. Sgt. Taxel told the Chetnik officer that the plane's radio receiver was not working at the time of their landing, but suggested that maybe the transmitter would work. The Chetnik officer assured the crew that in a matter of three or four days, they would be in Mihailovic held territory where the crew could be airlifted back to their base in Italy. Taking the Chetnik officer at his word, the entire crew felt relieved and that they would be back at their base in a week's time at most. Lt. Grossman still believed the Partisans were better suited to aid the crew in returning to their base but had no choice but to give the Chetniks a chance to make good on their promise. After all, he and his crew were in no position to bargain for their release to the Partisans. Doing so might only provoke the Chetniks.

By now the mood in the room changed to an even more optimistic view for the Americans. They began talking to one another about their predicament being an adventure that would make for an interesting conversation over a few beers with their buddies back at the base. Had the crew realized that their Chetnik friends promise of a return in a week turned out to be a gross understatement, they most certainly would not have been in such an adventurous mood.

In the corner of the main room of the Chetnik outpost, there was a large black pot warming over a small fire. The Chetnik officer offered the crew something to eat. The airmen gathered around a small table and with two men sharing a spoon due to a lack of eating utensils, they paired up in two's and took turns spooning out a type of a bean soup lacking in salt, with a piece of fatback thrown in. Not knowing when they might get their next meal, the crewmen wasted no time shoveling spoonful after spoonful of the broth down their throats. "It could sure use some salt" muttered Sgt. Baker. "Better than nothing Earl" whispered back Sgt. LeClair. After the men finished, Lt. Grossman spoke to the Chetnik Colonel. "How close are we to the Germans?" Col Junic replied, "The Germans occupy Banja Luca which is 10 to15 kilometers away. But they occasionally send out patrols into these mountains. And there are Ustachi in the area. Their sentries are mostly younger boys of sixteen or seventeen, but they will turn you in if you are spotted. If the Ustachi arrests you, you will not leave Yugoslavia alive! They are devils! Just like the Partisans" the Colonel added. He said this as though he hoped the mention of Partisans would have had as much of a negative effect on the Americans as the mention of the Germans or Ustachi. Lt. Grossman requested that he and one of his men be allowed to return to their plane to burn it. "That would be too dangerous!" said the Col. Junic. But Lt. Grossman persisted. "I must return to make sure anything on the plane of importance is recovered or destroyed along squadron markings before it falls into the hands of the Germans. It is my duty as pilot of the ship. I understand the danger, but I can assure you, we will be careful." he said. "The plane isn't that far from here. Perhaps Sgt. Bosko could lead us back to the plane."

Col. Junic asked Sgt. Bosko exactly where the plane crashed. Sgt. Bosko told him it was in a field only about two kilometers away. After a bit more discussion with Lt. Grossman and crew, the Colonel gave in. No one knows for sure why the Chetnik officer allowed Lt. Grossman to return to the plane to destroy it.

The speculation is that the Chetniks wanted to show the Americans that by complying with them, it would prove their loyalty to the Allies. They believed this was an important component to the relationship with the West when the Allied landing could take place in their country to defeat the occupying Nazis and perhaps block a communist takeover. But in truth, the Western Allies had no intention of landing boots on Yugoslavian soil and instead deferred any such landing to the Soviets. The Western Allies were more concerned with Western Europe's liberation from the Nazi's than they were of the Communists control of Yugoslavia. If the Western Allies had tried a landing on countries in the Balkans, it could quite possibly lead to another World War, this time with the Soviets. Without knowledge of the Allies intent after Germany's defeat, many Chetniks were hopeful that the Allies would help them by lending their support in the fight against the Communists once they defeated the Fascists. However, there were others in the Chetnik ranks who felt that the Allies had already betrayed them by ceasing to order supply drops so they could fight the Nazis. Instead, the drops of supplies were parachuted to the Partisan territories. The reasons for this change in support was that the British were in charge of giving the order to all Allied supply drops in the region. The Allies were worried about the Chetniks losing more territory to the Germans. On the other hand, the Partisans were making more advances against the German forces in the country. They were also getting several reports from operatives in Yugoslavia that many Chetniks were now fighting side by side with the Germans against Tito's Partisans. They thought that Draza Mihailovic, no longer had control and that the Chetniks were now being led by Nedic who was benefiting from the Nazis who were helping them in the fight against their hated Communists. Nedic believed the Allies had given up supporting the Chetniks and were giving more support to the Communist Partisans. This belief allowed Nedic to rally a large portion of Chetniks and convince them to comply with the Germans to defeat a common enemy in the Communists. But as for Mihailovic, he did not waver in his support for the Allies despite the split in the Chetnik leadership. Mihailovic's Chetniks stayed loyal to the Allies. From a political view, he knew he had to order his ranks to continue helping downed American airmen or risk losing the hopeful support of the Western Allies in his continuing a fight against the Communists after the Nazis were defeated.

Colonel Junic was a "Mihailovic" Chetnik, and that was very fortunate for the crew, though some of his subordinates were less than cheerful towards their American guests. But they followed orders no matter what their attitude towards the crew was. The Germans tried to sway some Chetniks over to their side. They even offered the Chetniks three cents for any downed Allied airmen turned over to them. To a Chetnik, three cents was about a days wage. It is unknown for sure if any of the Chetnik escorts or soldiers who were sheltering the crew were tempted to turn the crew into the Germans for a payoff. But in the days to come, it became apparent to the crew, that their escorts were quite aware of the Nazi's offer. But no matter how tempting, turning the American crew over to the Germans would run the risk of facing serious reprisals from not only the Mihailovic supporting Chetniks but worse, they could be captured by the advancing Communist Partisans.

As the first evening of the airmen's crash landing wore on, Lt. Grossman informed his crew that he needed to return to the plane to see that it would be set afire before the Germans discovered it. He asked Sgt. LeClair if he'd volunteer to go along with him and a Chetnik as an escort. "Sure, I'll go with you Lieutenant," said his flight engineer. "OK fine" said Lt. Grossman. "Let's go Sgt. The rest of you fellas sit tight till we get back." "Are you sure about going out there?" asked Lt. Daniels.

"Don't worry, at the first sign of trouble, we'll call it off and return" replied Lt. Grossman. Colonel Junic then reluctantly ordered one of his men to guide the two Americans back to the crash site. He warned the escort to scout ahead and to take charge and return if it became too dangerous, no matter what the American Lieutenant insisted.

Colonel Junic then made sure that Lt. Grossman understood that his escort must be obeyed at all cost. Lt. Grossman agreed but was determined to carry out the military order he learned during pilot training.

## Chapter 7

The night was cold and dark and with only a sliver of the moon in the sky. Their Chetnik escort led Lt. Grossman and Sgt. LeClair to the crash site. It was hard for the two airmen to notice the pathway to their plane because of the darkness, but their escort was careful to avoid any main trails and made sure they stayed out of sight by keeping within the treeline for cover. When they arrived at their crashed bomber in the snow covered potato field, Lt. Grossman and Sgt. LeClair climbed on board while the Chetnik escort stood watch. The men quickly began looking for anything that would burn, like rubber oxygen masks or hose lines. Then they stepped outside and walked over the wings and tried to see where they could ignite the wing fuel tanks, even though there were only fumes left. Knowing they had to act fast, Lt. Grossman and Sgt. LeClair took out their lighters and went back inside the bomber and set fire to whatever would burn. Soon after, a fire within the fuselage of the plane came to life. Unfortunately, someone about a hundred yards away noticed the flickering of light. It was another small group of Chetnik soldiers that appeared from a nearby farm. Lt. Grossman and Sgt. LeClair's Chetnik escort recognized the Serbian fighters as they approached. He explained that he was ordered to escort the American airmen to their plane so they could burn it before the Germans discovered it. The Chetnik group's leader said that the Ustachi was in the area and that the fire might draw their unwanted attention. They didn't wait for a second longer and began putting out the on board fire by scattering snow over the small flames as Lt. Grossman, Sgt. LeClair and their escort scampered off to avoid a possible capture by the Ustachi and hiked back to the Chetnik outpost. They arrived about an hour later. "What happened Bob? Did you burn the ship?" asked Lt. Keane as he and the rest of the crew were roused awake.

"We tried to. We started a fire on board and were ready to head back when along comes some other group of Chetnik renegades who put out the fire. They thought we might get spotted by the enemy, but the only people we saw were these Chetniks" replied Lt. Grossman. As Lt. Grossman was talking to his men, the Chetnik escort was explaining what happened to Col. Junic who seemed relieved about the failed attempt. By now, Lt. Grossman and Sgt. LeClair were exhausted and after things settled down Col. Junic suggested they all get some sleep. With that, Lieutenants Grossman, Escardo, Daniels and Keane and Sargents Gourley,

LeClair, Sparks, Taxel, Baker, and White settled in for the night while their Chetnik escorts took turns keeping watch just outside the front entrance of the small stone outpost.

The next morning, the crew were awakened by one of the Chetnik soldiers. The crew started sitting up from the beds of straw piled on the floor where they were sleeping. Sgt. Gourley looked around for his harness and noticed that his G.I. land boots that were tied to the harness were missing! Sgt. Gourley looked around and said "Hey! Which one of you fellas stole my boots!" "Probably one of them took them during the night" replied Sgt. Sparks are pointing towards the door where the Chetnik guards stood posted. Most Chetniks soldiers had the most primitive footwear at best. Any decent pair of boots not being worn was fair game! Sgt. Gourley took a peek at the two Chetnik guards posted outside, but neither were wearing American made GI boots. Knowing it would be futile to accuse any of the guards of theft, Sgt. Gourley could only dwell on the fact that any traveling on foot would have to be done while wearing his bulky, uncomfortable flying boots.

After a small portion of bean soup for breakfast, it only left the crew longing for the powdered eggs they had loathed back at their base. Col Junic informed the crew that they would have to sit tight for a couple of days while they organized with other outposts that would relay the crew eventually to Mihailovic's headquarters. After arriving there, preparations for an airlift would be arranged. Lt. Grossman had a word with his crew and again made it clear that the plane MUST be burned. "We need to go back to that field and burn the plane," said Lt. Grossman. "We should all go together this time," said Lt. Escardo. Believing that with the crew staying together this time, it would be good for morale, Lt. Grossman agreed. Col. Junic was consulted, and again he protested, but finally agreed as long as they stayed with the Chetnik escorts at all times. That afternoon, after a couple of miles hiking back to the crash site, the crew and their escorts came upon their B-17 resting in several feet of snow. Lt. Grossman ordered his crew to join him and start the process of setting the bomber on fire as quickly as possible. As the men got closer to the plane, they found the local farmers had heavily stripped it. "There's hardly anything left to burn" remarked Sgt. LeClair to Sgt. Baker with a bit of sarcasm. Things like the wing panels were missing as well as parts of the fuselage including the escape hatch doors. Lt. Grossman approached Sgt. Taxel. "Sargent, ask Bosko why was the plane stripped." Sgt.

Taxel asked Sgt. Bosko using his German language skills and translated back to Lt. Grossman. "From what I can understand Lieutenant, he says the farmers will use everything they can from the plane, especially the metal from the wings. They will use them for roofs, gates, rain gutters …anything they can find a use for." Apparently to the farmers in the area, aluminum was as precious as gold! A few of the crew were successful in igniting some of the more combustible items still on board including setting a fire in the cockpit in the hopes of destroying the instrument panel. Aided by traces of fuel vapors in the fuel lines, the plane's remains slowly began burning, much to the satisfaction of Lt. Grossman. The escorts then hurried the crew back to the outpost.

The speculation as to why Col. Junic would again allow the crew to return to the crash site for a second attempt to burn their plane, is that although the task risked detection, the location of the crash was in a relatively safe zone occupied by mostly Serbian farmers who were sympathetic to the Allies. Many Chetnik guerrilla fighters were sons of these farmers and lived in these farmhouses. And also it was the winter season. Had it been the summer, Lt. Grossman's order to burn the plane would have been out of the question. In the warmer season, the farms in the area were raided several times by the Germans. They would take most of the farmer's crop where it was used to feed the soldiers of the German Army. But in the winter season, the Germans rarely ventured up into the mountain farmland. Another advantage of the cold winter weather was that all the farmhouses in the area were constantly burning wood in their fireplaces for heat. With smoke rising from all the farmhouses in the area, the thought was another smoke rise wouldn't look suspicious to the Germans based in the low country. While some Ustachis were in the area, they were positioned at checkpoints along the roads near the outskirts of towns on orders from their Nazi superiors. And most of these Ustachi roadblocks were manned by younger teenage boys. Still, a danger if spotted. The crash site was secure for the moment, but the crew would soon learn that they would eventually have to be guided through territory that would require great effort to avoid being spotted at the checkpoints which could lead to being captured and subjected to torture and inevitable execution by the superiors of the dreaded and brutal Ustachi.

The crew spent their second night in Yugoslavia at the outpost they were taken to after crash landing. The next morning, Col. Junic gathered the Americans and spoke to them. "Tonight, you all will be moved to another location." After sunset on January 24th, the crew assembled for the trek to the next relay outpost. Lt. Grossman and the rest of the crew were somewhat in an upbeat mood hoping they would soon be relayed to a safe location and be airlifted back to Italy.

Col. Junic called for a detachment of three Chetnik soldiers that included Sgt. Bosko and a couple of horse-driven sleighs to guide them. It was cold and overcast making it an even darker night. Sgt. Bosko would lead the crew by sleigh for part of the journey. He sent one of the escorts ahead as a scout. If the scout were to spot any Ustachis or Germans, he was to return to the line, and they would abort making contact with the other Chetnik group. But Sgt. Bosko seemed more concerned about running into Partisans. He didn't speak much during the journey, but when he did, it was mostly to warn the crew to be quiet because Partisans were nearby. After a few hours heading southeast on the sleighs, they came upon the Vrbas River. Vbras , meaning "willow" because of the abundance of willow trees that line its banks in and around the city of Banja Luca. Fortunately, the portion of the river they had to cross was still frozen. As they proceeded to cross it, the crew could hear the ice below cracking below the sleighs. It was only a short time after they crossed the river that they met up with some other Chetniks. Sgt. Bosko had the crew dismount the sleighs. He now would lead them on foot because the trail became too narrow and hazardous to travel by sleigh higher up the mountain. The other Chetniks took the sleighs back in the other direction. Now on foot, the crew and their escorts marched on up the mountain trail. After midnight they took a brief rest in a small deserted barn the Chetniks used for shelter from time to time. It was quite a relief to get out of the cold if even for a moment to thaw out.

Sgt. Sparks said to Sgt. Gourley, "I wonder how much longer we have to go?" "I don't know, but I sure wish I had my GI boots! It's hard enough walking in these damn flying boots!" After their rest break, Sgt. Bosko motioned for the crew to continue. The mountain trails were not very wide, so the crew marched two by two and at times single file, with Sgt. Bosko in front and the other Chetniks at the rear of the crew. They were traveling south by southeast bypassing Banja Luca to the west which was occupied by the Germans. The crew had been marching all night long in the cold winter chill and were completely exhausted when just as the sun was rising, Sgt. Bosko pointed to a farm about a half mile in the distance on a neighboring hillside. The crew had reached the outskirts of the small farming village one and a half miles east of the town of Celinac,(pronounced Che-lee-nas) which is about three miles southeast of Banja Luca.  The second outpost was just another Chetnik safe house located on the other side of the valley.

Lt. Grossman was expecting a small cabin-like structure similar to the first outpost. Or worse yet, a more primitive place, like perhaps a mountain cave! Soon the group arrived at the farm. Sgt. Bosko approached an older looking man standing beside the small front gate attached to a tattered picket fence leading to his farmhouse. The two began talking while the crew stood back with the other Chetnik escorts. Soon Sgt. Bosko motioned for the crew to approach. In German Sgt. Bosko said to Sgt. Taxel who translated, "This is where you will stay for now. I need to make contact with my comrades who are across the valley. They have your plane's radio. But to get there, we must go down into the valley and cross the river where the Germans and Ustachi are camped. It is too dangerous right now." The Ustachi's set up a roadblock nearby the trail to the second Chetnik outpost. This would require a bit of re-thinking up an alternate trail the crew could be taken. As the Americans walked through the open front gate, the crew were greeted one by one by the farmer. "Dobrodosli" (Welcome!) he said to each man with a broad smile. The farmer's name was Dragutin Cvijanovic. He was fifty-one years old, a fairly tall and slim Serbian man with short graying hair with a strong, rugged face that made him look ten years older. He lived there with his wife, fifty-two-year-old Vasilia, and their six children. Three sons, Momchilo (the youngest at ten years of age), Milorad (12) and Mico (16). And three daughters Mira (18), Stevka,(15) and Dobrila (20). He impressed the crew with his warm hospitality. He acted almost as though he were expecting the Americans…which in fact he was not. But as an Orthodox Christian who despised the Nazis and their puppet police, the Ustachi, he understood the importance of preventing the American airmen from falling into the hands of the Germans or the Ustachi. Sgt. Bosko knew of  Mr. Cvijanovic for some time because the old farmer served as mayor of Celinac from 1920 to 1938 and he was well known in the vicinity of Banja Luca and the neighboring towns and mountain villages. Mr. Cvijanovic had a well-respected reputation throughout this region. Many Chetniks held him in high regard. He had once hidden a Jewish family at his farm in 1941 during the German occupation before turning them over to an underground unit, which helped the family get out of Yugoslavia. No one ever learned of what became of that family, but Sgt. Bosko assured the Americans that the farmer could be trusted. This stop was planned to be the first of the relay to eventual freedom, or so they hoped.

Dragutin Cvijanovic was also known his for diplomatic abilities among his Serbian neighbors and even some of the Croatians when he lived among them before the war. The local population not only the feared the potential Nazi or Ustachi reprisals for harboring downed allied airmen, but also serious reprisals at the hands of the Communist Tito's Partisans who viewed the Chetniks as enemies. The Partisans wanted no part in allowing the Chetniks to take credit for rescuing any downed allied airmen. Though Lt. Grossman and the rest of the crew were briefed about the Partisans being better equipped to rescue them, at least for the time being, they were kept unaware of Dragutin's plight should the Partisans ever discover his harboring allied airmen. He also knew deep down that Sgt. Bosko or any of the Chetniks in the area could not get the crew to Mihailovic's headquarters. For the time being, he kept this fact from the crew as well. Dragutin feared that telling the crew would only cause friction between the crew and their Chetnik escorts perhaps leading to an act made in haste that might bring harm to either side. Dragutin knew he would eventually have to inform the crew about their Chetnik escorts but now was not the time. For now, Dragutin would do his best to see that his American guests were well cared for.

No one particular area of the local landscape was perfectly safe from the Germans and Ustachi patrols, but for the moment his farm was in a relatively safe zone. The Germans and Ustachi were in one sector, the Partisans were in the opposite sector leaving his farm generally in the middle, but higher up in the mountains. By late 1944 as the battlefront closed in, it worked in Dragutin's favor because neither side wanted to venture up into the mountains without reason, especially in winter. And by now, the Ustachi had begun to lose control of the mountainous regions making it too difficult to carry out massacres in the smaller mountain villages of Serbian citizens. They would not venture up to the mountains without the German's support due to fear of a Chetnik ambush, but the German army could not spare any troops to help them carry out their type of madness on the civilians. So the Ustachis preferred patrolling the roads and trails that led to and from the mountain region, although the Germans had no problem heading up to the farm and helping themselves to the Cvijanovic's summer crops of corn, wheat, and potatoes when crops were in harvest season. It is quite possible that because of their need for his crops, the Germans let him be and ordered the Ustachis to do the same. Of course, the Germans still pillaged most of their crops leaving his family just enough to survive. But the Germans made sure that Mr. Cvijanovic knew who ruled the land. For example in late summer or early fall 1942 after the Jewish family had left, the Germans had come up to the mountain and burned down Dragutin's barn to send a message, but not before taking most of their livestock of sheep, pigs and cows and, of course, the crops of the harvest. It was a typical show of intimidation by the German army towards the local population of territories they occupied. If the Germans had no use for Mr. Cvijanovic and his harvest, they might set fire to more structures than his barn. And if they knew he had harbored any Jews or enemies of the Third Reich, such as allied airmen, they most certainly would have executed him and his family.

Sgt. Bosko spoke to Dragutin and explained that he eventually needed to move the crew to another Chetnik outpost when it was safe and that they were going to rest and be on their way in a day or two. But despite the enormous risk, Dragutin suggested that the Americans stay with him indefinitely because of the strong presence of Germans and Utstachis in Celinac and that the Americans would be safer in his mountain farmhouse. Sgt. Bosko agreed for the time being since he was in no mood to tangle with the Germans. Lt. Escardo asked if Dragutin could speak Italian since he could. Dragutin replied in Italian that he could but was more familiar with German since he used it regularly when Austria had occupied Yugoslavia before World War I. Lt. Grossman asked Sgt. Taxel to again act as translator. After entering the house and spending the time learning more about each crew member, the afternoon turned to evening. While the Chetnik escorts stood "guard" outside, Mrs. Cvijanovic motioned for the men to gather for a meal. She had prepared one chicken for dinner. The fact that Mr. And Mrs. Cvijanovic could have saved the chicken for another meal with their children only goes to prove just how generous they were. Mrs. Cvijanovic made sure everyone, the American airmen, and her family, received a small portion of meat. She also served a small portion of field corn and boiled a couple of potatoes. To say that the food was scarce is an understatement. But this illustrates that Mrs.Cvijanovic knew just how much food to dole out to keep everyone fed. After the meal, the three Cvijanovic daughters cleaned up after the men, not allowing any of their American guests to so much as clear any dish from the table. As the women cleaned up after dinner, the men still gathered around the table, Mr. Cvijanovic broke out a bottle of fruit brandy called Rakia, much to the interest of the crew. Made mostly from plums, Rakia was one of the more popular alcoholic drinks in the region. After a toast to his American guests, the men began a more serious conversation about their situation. Sgt. Taxel was again using his knowledge of German, therefore, acting as translator. Mr. Cvijanovic briefed the crew on their present situation and the difficult political situation going on in the country. Lt. Grossman spoke up. "Can you help us get out of the country safely?" "It is too dangerous to move you right now" responded Mr. Cvijanovic. He continued, "I have told Sgt. Bosko that it might be best if you stay here for a while as he and his comrades prepare a plan to get you out to Mihailovic, headquarters." "What about the Partisans?" asked Lt. Grossman. "I cannot deliver you to the Partisans. You see, I'm considered a Chetnik myself. The Partisan Communists are our enemy. They would arrest me immediately if they were to find out I was harboring Americans." responded Mr. Cvijanovic. As the crew listened to every word of Sgt. Taxels' translation, they began to chime in. "We can't stay here for long," said Lt. Keane. "Yea, and what if the Germans are looking for us" added Lt. Daniels. "Tomorrow I will go into the village and see if it the Germans are indeed looking for you." replied Mr. Cvijanovic. Mr. Cvijanovic was not a collaborator, but since the Germans had bigger fish to fry, for instance, the Partisans, they pretty much let the Chetniks pass through town, especially Chetnik soldiers since they were in a battle with the Partisans who were making serious advances on the German army in Yugoslavia. The Ustachis were a different bunch. They would pose a much bigger threat for Mr. Cvijanovic and any of the Chetnik escorts if stirred by any suspicious activity. But since Mr. Cvijanovic was known to many locals of different political factions since before the more recent Croation and Serbian uprising and because his farm was useful to the Germans as a food source, the Nazi-backed Ustachi may have held off keeping a closer eye on his routines while in town. But if the Cvijanovics were ever caught harboring any allied airmen, just like being arrested by the Nazis, it would mean certain death for the entire family. So the risk Mr. Cvijanovic was taking was tremendous. He was well aware of the risk, yet he felt compelled to help the crew. It also helped that he took an instant liking to the American airmen.

After a while, Mr. Cvijanovic decided it was time to turn in. He retired to the main bedroom while his wife prepared the main room for the crew to sleep. The children occupied the outside shed except for the youngest boy, Momchilo, who slept at the foot of his parent's bed to keep his Father's feet warm. This selfless act by the youngster made quite an impression on the crew, particularly Sgt. Taxel. He thought it was quite a display of a young boy's devotion to his Father. Sgt. Bosko and his fellow Chetnik escort occupied another smaller shed each taking turns guarding the main house throughout the night. The crew would sleep on beds of straw on the floor close to the fire. Lt. Grossman and his crew all found a place to lie. With freezing temperatures outside it was quite a sight as the crew was maneuvering to get as close to the fireplace as possible to keep warm. By morning, Mrs. Cvijanovic came out of her bedroom fully dressed and quietly chuckled seeing that the American airmen were practically "spooning" neatly in a row in front of the fireplace. Mr. Cvijanovic appeared, the children came into the house, and the crew was awakened to join the family for breakfast that resembled something like porridge, but tasted more like sawdust! Soon after, Sgt. Bosko and the other Chetnik soldier entered the house and engaged in some Serbian small talk. The girls went on with their chores including chopping firewood while the boys tended to the farm. After a while, Sargents Gourley and White went outside and insisted on helping the girls with chopping the firewood. Sgt. Gourley approached Stevka Cvjaniovic. "Can I help you with the firewood?" Stevka and her sisters Mira and Dobrila looked at Sgt. Gourley with puzzled faces. "We'd like to help you chop the firewood," said Sgt. White as he was miming an impersonation of someone chopping wood. Stevka smiled and upon recognizing Sgt. White's gesture said "Da, Havala !"(Yes, Thank you!). As White and Gourley started chopping firewood, the rest of the crew began milling about outside the main farmhouse. The Chetnik guards stood by watching and smoking crudely made cigarettes. They were waiting for word from their superior officer for the next move for the airmen.

## Chapter 8

Later in the afternoon, two more Chetnik soldiers arrived at the farm. They told the Americans to assemble. It was time to move on. Before they knew it, the crew were led off by the Chetnik escorts. These Chetnik soldiers were to be the first in a series of relay escorts that would eventually take the crew to Mihailovic's headquarters in Pranjani. A few hours into their hike, one of the Chetnik escorts spotted two men crossing the trail about 20 yards ahead. Before the Chetnik could react, Lt. Daniels recognized them as wearing USAAF flight suits and said, "Hey, those guys are Americans!" The two men turned to look back to see the ten crewmen crew walking towards them. At first, the Chetnik escorts drew their weapons thinking they might be Partisans, but then relaxed their rifles after many in the crew told the Chetniks, "Don't shoot, don't shoot, they're Americans!" After confirming they were among friendlies, the two airmen looked at the crew coming towards them with a great sigh of relief. At first, they thought the crew was a platoon of Germans. They were encouraged to join the march and readily accepted knowing that they were among fellow Americans. The Chetnik escorts told the men they must keep moving so they could reach the next relay point on schedule. While marching, Lt. Grossman introduced himself and the crew. "I'm first pilot Lt. Grossman.  This is Lieutenants Escardo, Keane, Daniels and Sargents LeClair, Taxel, Gourley, Sparks, Baker, and White. What is your name airman?" One of the airmen replied in a noticeable southern drawl, "I'm Sargent Larry Whetstone, and this is Corporal Robert Howe, sir." "What group are you men with" asked Lt. Grossman. "We're with the 484th Bomb group sir," replied Sgt. Whetstone. "About a week ago our B-24 took several flak hits on a mission to Wiener-Neudorf (Austria). We had already dropped our bomb load and were heading home when the 88's and 105 flak guns opened up on the formation. We tried to make it back, but our pilot couldn't keep us airborne much longer, so he hit the bail out alarm. That's when we jumped. We came down a couple of miles from Celinac and were laying low in case the Germans were out looking for us," explained Sgt. Whetstone. "Where's the rest of your crew?  Did everyone bailout?" asked Lt. Grossman. " I think so Lieutenant" replied Cpl. Howe. "Larry and I were the first to jump. I saw a few more chutes leave the plane as I was coming down, but they drifted further south. We don't know what happened to the rest of the crew sir" added the

Corporal. "We spent the past week hiding out in an old barn at an abandoned farm, sir" said Sgt. Whetstone. "We were scouting the area hoping to run into some friendlies" Sgt. Whetstone added. "Lieutenant, are these soldiers Partisans?" "Keep your voice down Sargent. No. They're Chetniks - and don't mention the word "Partisans" within earshot of any Chetnik," Lt. Grossman said in a hushed voice. "Well sir, can these Chetniks get us back to our base?" Cpl. Howe asked. "I hope so Corporal" replied Lt. Grossman. He went on to say, "We're with the 483rd. We crash landed near Banja Luca a few days ago. I guess you guys are stuck with us" said Lt. Grossman. Sgt. White joined in the conversation. "Where're you boys from?" he asked. "Equality, Alabama," replied Sgt. Whetstone. "Reading, Massachusetts," added Cpl. Howe. As the men marched another mile or two, getting more acquainted with the two B-24 evaders, they came to an abrupt halt. One of the Chetnik's told the men to take cover in the brush while the other scouted ahead. This was their routine when they passed through the unchecked territory. The area they were in was constantly changing from friendly to unfriendly every few days, depending on the troop movement of each faction. One day it might be held by the Chetniks, the next day they would be pushed out, and it would be under German, and their ally Ustachi's control, or Tito's Communist Partisans might control the area.

So the Chetniks made it a point to send a scout ahead and make sure all was clear before proceeding at certain points on the trail. A few minutes passed when suddenly, the Chetnik scout came running up. He reported to the other Chetnik that they must return to the Cvijanovic's farm on the double. He then told the crew to keep quiet and there was a Ustachi patrol at a checkpoint about a half a mile down the trail! They all quickly turned around and headed back. They arrived safely back to the farm after their close call along with the two B-24 crewmen feeling disappointed that they failed to reach Pranjani so they could get evacuated as promised. Now the Cvijanovics had twelve American airmen to hide at their farm and two more mouths to feed. But not one word of complaint was heard by any member of the Cvijanovic family. They welcomed Sgt. Whetsone and Cpl. Howe just the same as they welcomed Lt. Grossman's crew.

A few days later, Mr. Cvijonovic and his sons left to visit a neighboring farm perhaps to trade something for more food and supplies. He told the crew he should return before dark. Sgt. Bosko arrived shortly after. He began talking with the two other Chetnik soldier/escorts and then walked over to Lt. Grossman. He explained that the Chetnik soldiers had their B-17's radio back at their outpost located on a deserted farm. He told him that his comrades were trying to fix the radio so they could make contact with the Mihailovics headquarters in Pranjani or perhaps the American's base in Italy to at least let them know that the crew was and safe in their care. By now the crew was certainly concerned about the MIA telegrams that would be sent out to their loved ones back home. They were quite aware of the effects these letters would have on their families receiving such a telegram. Any chance of getting a message about their condition out of Yugoslavia intrigued Lt. Grossman. He realized his wife Madeline would be sick with worry once she received the dreaded telegram. It only motivated him to find a way to make contact with his base in Italy. He asked Sgt. Bosko, "Can you take us with you to this other farm? Maybe our radioman can fix it?" "No….too dangerous to move you all right now" replied Sgt. Bosko. Sgt. Taxel spoke up "Lieutenant, what if they only take me? I could take a look at it at least?" Lt. Grossman and Sgt. Taxel turned to Sgt. Bosko to get his thoughts about a smaller detachment for the journey. "Well maybe, I could take one or two of your men." Finally, after much discussion on who should accompany Sgt. Taxel, Sgt. Sparks volunteered to go along. It was decided to leave after the sun went down. After dusk, Sgt. Bosko left with Sargents Taxel and Sparks while the other Chetnik escorts stayed behind. The rest of the crew retired to the farmhouse to join Mrs. Cvijanovic and her daughters and waited for Mr. Cvijanovic to return with his sons. After hiking down the mountain, Sgt. Bosko pulled the men off the trail, where hidden behind some trees, another Chetnik escort with a horse-driven sleigh was waiting for them. It was a common way to travel in winter among the local Chetniks. Having a horse driven sleigh on the snow covered terrain for use would save a lot of time and be used for carrying weapons and supplies, albeit in small quantities.

"Get in the sleigh" ordered Sgt. Bosko. "And stay quiet! Partisans close by." The two Americans hopped in the sleigh and were told to get in the back, stay down and hide beneath the blankets in the back. Sgt. Bosko rode in the front with the other Chetnik and off they went. They came upon the Vrbanja river which was frozen solid and crossed it. They could hear the ice cracking below them, praying that they would get to the other side without crashing into the icy river. Safely across they headed back up the other side of the valley where the trail took them to the empty farm the Chetniks had brought the B-17's radio. Sargents Taxel and

Sparks were taken to the barn and they were greeted by more Chetniks. There they saw the radio and also some of the planes .50 machine guns with their ammo belts!

Meanwhile back at the Cvijanovic's, Mr. Cvijanovic arrived back home from his visit with his neighbor's farm and was quite upset when he learned Sgt. Taxel and Sgt Sparks had departed for the other side of the valley. In his Serbian language he ranted on something to the effect as paraphrased, "If the Germans or Ustachi discover your men, they will not only arrest them, they will come and arrest my family and me! It is VERY dangerous!" he continued. Lt. Grossman didn't know how to respond because he couldn't understand Mr. Cvijanovic, but he knew the old man was very angry. With the help of Lt. Escardo, who could speak a bit of Italian which Mr. Cvijanovic understood.  He tried to explain that as leader of the crew, it was his duty to find a way to make contact with his superiors at his airbase if given a chance. After his outburst, the house became very quiet. The men gathered to eat, as Mrs. Cvijanovic doled out a small portion of soup for the crew and her family, and then they all retired for the night. Lt. Daniels said,"I hope the guys make out ok?" "If they do, we will know soon enough" quipped Lt. Keane. Meanwhile Sargents Taxel and Sparks spent the night at the Chetnik farm/outpost trying to get their plane's radio to work but it was useless without an adequate power source and parts needed to get it working properly.

The next morning, the two American crewmen awoke to the news from a couple of arriving Chetniks that it was too dangerous to move Taxel and Sparks back to Mr. Cvijanovic's farm. Some of the German army, who were fighting the Partisans, were retreating along the trails the men had traveled the day before. They would have to wait until the coast was clear. Finally, after two more days at the farm outpost, a Chetnik soldier arrived from the valley in the morning and told them the Germans were now clear of the trails for the time being. The two Americans could be moved back to Mr. Cvjanovic's farm and rejoin the rest of their crew. But there was one problem -- a big problem. The weather had warmed up a bit the day before. The soldier told Sgt. Bosko that the ice on the Vrbanja river that Taxel and Sparks were taken across by sleigh just a couple of days earlier, had broken up, making it impossible to cross. The only way back now would be for the party to travel through the Nazi occupied city of Banja Luca and then backtrack toward the town of Celinac. The Chetniks couldn't possibly take Taxel and Sparks dressed in their USAAF flight suits and not go unnoticed by the Germans.  After careful thought,

Sgt. Bosko came up with a plan. He knew that the Germans were not as concerned as in the past when the Chetniks challenged the Nazi occupation in 1941. To recap, by 1944-45 the Germans found the Chetniks useful in their fight against the Communist Partisans and vice verse. As long as the Sgt. Bosko's party appeared headed to the battlefront against the Partisans, they should be able to make it through Banja Luca without much threat by the Germans. The real threat would be the Ustachi's near Celinac. But Sgt. Bosko knew some back trails he hoped they could use to avoid any Ustachi roadblocks on the outskirts of the town. So Sgt. Bosko planned to have the two Americans change out of their flight suits and into Chetnik uniforms borrowed from a couple of not too enthusiastic Chetnik guerrilla fighters. As the Chetnik soldiers changed out of their soldier's garb and into civilian clothes they wore as farmhands, the American airmen changed into the Chetniks uniforms. Sgt. Bosko told Sgt.s Taxel and Sparks to hide their flight suits in the back of the sleigh and they could change back into them once they reached the Cvijanovic's farm. Taxel and Sparks both climbed in the sleigh dressed as Chetnik guerrilla fighters ready for battle complete with belts of ammo crisscrossing their chest, hand grenades, and automatic weapons. Sgt. Bosko even took along one of the B-17's .50 caliber machine guns and hid it down at his feet. He rode in the back with Taxel and Sparks while another Chenik escort drove the sleigh. Both Taxel and Sparks were nervous about changing uniforms because if discovered by the German's, they would be considered spies and executed on the spot. Sgt. Bosko convinced them that this was the only way to get back to the Cvijanovic's farm. With everyone on board, the Chetnik smacked the leather reigns on the horses' backside and off they went.

They were traveling north towards Banja Luca about four miles away, paralleling the Vrbanja river to the east and the larger Vrbas river to the west. After a while, they arrived in Banja Luca. Sgt. Bosko told Taxel and Sparks to keep quiet and let him do the talking should they get stopped. He avoided the center of town where most of the Germans were occupying. But just as Sgt. Bosko had predicted, the few German soldiers they passed in town paid little attention to the uniformed "Chetniks" in the sleigh. No one on the sleigh ever thought or mentioned the possibility that had any German sentry wanted to stop them, he most assuredly would have spotted the American made .50 caliber machine gun lying at the feet of Sgt. Bosko. Their cover most certainly would have been blown. Turning onto a snow covered road, they passed a small two-story building and saw a horrific sight.

They looked up and saw a man hung by a rope wrapped around a four-by-four piece of wood attached to a telegraph pole just outside the corner of the building. The man's neck was stretched and his motionless dead body was dangling high above the ground. Sgt. Bosko turned to Taxel and Sparks and pointed to his neck and said to them, "This is what will happen to me if I get caught aiding American airmen" He then made a slash gesture across his throat.

They soon crossed one of the small narrow bridges over the Vrbanja river. A short time after they crossed the river, they came to a fork in the trail. A left turn would lead them northwest towards the main road that the Germans were using to retreat or resupply from the battlefront with the Partisans to the south. A right turn would take them south towards Celinac and eventually the Cvjnanovic's farm. The sleigh driver turned and headed south. They would appear to any passing column of Germans that they were a group of Chetnik guerrilla fighters heading to the front to fight the Communists.  Now the sleigh was backtracking towards Celinac. The Ustachis had set up roadblocks on the outskirts of town to check anyone passing through, in or out of Celinac. Sgt. Bosko hoped to avoid the roadblock by using the back trail he had planned on using. Things were looking good so far. They avoided drawing attention by the Germans in Banja Luca. No one was following them on the southern route towards Celinac. They turned on to the snow covered back trail. Taxel and Sparks were looking forward to getting back to the rest of the crew even though they had no good news regarding their attempt to repair the radio enough to transmit any messages regarding their status. They were within a few hundred yards before ditching the sleigh and hiking up the mountain to the Cvijanovic's farm when he saw a Ustachi roadblock suddenly appear as they came around a bend in the road. Unbeknownst to Sgt. Bosko, the Ustachis had recently set up a roadblock on the less traveled back trail. Speculation is that Ustachi were ordered by the Nazis to set up more roadblocks as an early warning system to alert them to enemy advancement. The German Vermacht believed the Partisans were planning on using these backtrails to surround the town of Celinac, eventually. The sentries were their early warning should a Partisan column be spotted. And they could snare evading downed American airmen.  Sargents Taxel and Sparks thought this was it for them! As the sleigh came closer, two Ustachi sentries in their black uniforms resembling that of the Nazi's Gestapo unit, put out their hands and yelled "HALT!" The Ustachi sentries looked to be no more than sixteen or seventeen years of age. They ordered the men to dismount. Leaving their weapons in the sleigh, Taxel and Sparks climbed out of the sleigh first followed by the Chetnik escort who was driving the sleigh. No doubt they knew as soon as they said a word, they would be arrested and shot as spies. As the Ustachi sentries approached, Sgt. Bosko still seated in the sleigh, suddenly picked up the B-17's .50 caliber machine gun and pointed it, handheld, at the two stunned Ustachi soldiers and in Serbian yelled: "Odlozite oruzje I ruke u vis!" ("Drop your weapons and put your hands up!") The two Ustachi's stood frozen with their hands stretching skyward. Sgt. Bosko told Taxel, Sparks and the other Chetnik to grab the flight suits quickly. He then told the Chetnik escort to go ahead without him. He would catch up later. The three of them took off up the mountain in the direction of the Cvijanovic's farm. No one knows for sure what became of the Ustachis' sentries. But based on the historical climate of the times in Yugoslavia, it is most likely they did not survive this encounter. It is probable that Sgt. Bosko took them prisoner and turned them over to his Chetnik comrades who would have executed them in an act of retaliation for the many Serbs that were executed by Ustachi.

It was late in the afternoon when Sargents Taxel and Sparks, led by the Chetnik escort, arrived back at the Cvijanovic's farm. They were met by Mr. Cvijanovic who was still very upset at them and the Chetnik escort for putting his family and the rest of the crew at risk. With Taxel and Sparks still dressed in their Chetnik uniforms, Sargents Baker, LeClair, White and Gourley were all smiles, laughing and slapping the two on their backs in joyous relief the two crewmen were alright. Sgt. Sparks said, "Stan, you got to get a picture of me in this getup! Go get your camera," he said. Sgt. Taxel entered the farmhouse and looked for the box camera he brought with him on the mission. He came back out of the house with the camera in hand and had Sgt. Sparks pose for the picture. "Smile," said Sgt. Taxel as he took a picture of Sgt. Sparks standing at attention in the Chetnik uniform, holding the large automatic weapon at his side. "I hope that picture turns out alright." said Sgt. Sparks. "I won't know for sure until we get home," said Sgt. Taxel. "Unless you know someone in this territory with a dark room," he joked. Sounding more serious, Lt. Grossman ordered the men to settle down. He asked Taxel and Sparks, "What are you guys doing dressed like Chetniks? Where are your flight uniforms?" Right here sir" responded Sgt. Sparks as he dropped his bundled up flight suit on the table. "The ice broke up, so we were forced to go through Banja Luca. We needed the uniforms to blend in and avoid being spotted by any of the Germans in town Lieutenant" replied Sgt. Taxel. "Well, you men better get out of those clothes and get back in your flight suits on the double" ordered Lt. Grossman. "You don't want to get shot as spies if the Germans decide to drop by" he added. Taxel and Sparks entered the tool shed and changed back into their USAAF flight suits. Meanwhile, Mr. Cvijanovic was speaking to the Chetnik escort who was collecting the Chetnik uniforms from Taxel and Sparks. In a quiet but serious tone, Mr. Cvijanovic was expressing anger at the young Chetnik for his and Sgt. Bosko's part in putting his family in danger. The Chetnik escort was seemingly telling the nervous head of the house that everything was OK. Sgt. Taxel walked over and joined in speaking German to Mr. Cvjianovic. He was attempting to reassure him that no one had followed them to the farm. Meanwhile Lt. Escardo was curiously looking over the automatic weapon that Sgt. Sparks leaned near the front door of the house. "Where did you get this weapon?" he asked in his thick Peruvian accent. "It's a long story Lieutenant" replied an exhausted Sgt. Sparks. "What happened to you two? You were gone three days!" said Lt. Daniels. "Yeah, we were getting quite worried that you two got picked up by the Germans," added Lt. Keane. Then Taxel and Sparks briefed Lt. Grossman and the rest of the crew on the details of their three days away, including the inability to fix the radio, their brush with the Ustachi and Sgt. Bosko's bravery. That evening, the crew were treated to a dinner consisting of a single chicken that Mrs. Cvijanovic had killed and prepared for everyone to eat. It was the only chicken left on the farm to eat. This sharing of food demonstrated just how generous the Cvijanovic's were towards their American guests. Of course, the portions were very small, but for the first time since the crew crashed, they got to taste some real food. At times, they had to eat rotted goat meat. The Cvijanovic's were accustomed to eating the goat meat long after it had spoiled since food was scarce. Sometimes they would use the bones to make a broth. It was very hard on the crew's stomachs, but they managed to endure it. Although some of the crew, like Sgt. Baker, had a tougher time with the meals.

Lt. Grossman asked Sgt. Taxel to ask Mr. Cvijanovic if he could lead the men to the battlefront where perhaps they could seek help from the Partisans in getting the crew back to Italy. A full week had gone by and Lt. Grossman was bent on getting he and his crew back to their unit, whether that help came from the Chetniks or the Partisans. But Mr. Cvjanovic told Lt. Grossman that the best thing for the Americans would be to be patient and that he would go into Celinac every day and give them a full report on Ustachi activity and German troop movements. The next day the Americans stayed at the farm as another Chetnik soldier arrived to watch the crew to make sure they would stay put. Mr. Cvijanovic went into town as promised.

Sgt. Gourley was helping one of the Cvjanovic daughters by chopping up some firewood, while Sargent's LeClair and Sparks were tossing the younger boys Momchilo and Milorad into a pile of snow, much to the boy's enjoyment. Lieutenant's Keane and Daniels were busy making a snowman for the younger daughter Dobrilla who had never seen one or anything like it made from snow. Lt. Escardo and Lt. Grossman were chatting among themselves when suddenly, they heard the faint rumbling sound of piston engines in the sky high above. "Are those "seventeen's or twenty-four's?" wondered Lt. Daniels out loud. "Who cares which planes, they're Americans for sure!" said Lt. Keane. Quickly, Lt. Grossman ordered the men to join him in spelling out S.O.S. in the snow in open field adjacent to the farmhouse. They all began gathering some nearby tree branches and some logs of the firewood Sgt. Gourley was chopping.  Just as they finished the last "S" the men began yelling and waving to the bomber formation as they flew directly over the Cvijanovic's farm. But to no avail. These bombers were heading southwest back towards the Adriatic coast and across to Italy. "I'd give anything to be up there with those boys right now," said Sgt. White "Yea, heading home to a hot meal and a decent bed to lie in" added Sgt. Baker.

The crew watched as the last of the formation drifted out of sight, and slowly walked back to the farmhouse. Sgt. Gourley and Sgt. LeClair joined the newcomers, Sgt. Whetstone and Cpl. Howe, and picked up the fire logs and stacked them with the rest of the firewood, but they left the imprint in the snow along with the branches used to spell out their "SOS." The Chetnik escort seemed relieved the American bombers had not spotted the crews' attempt to be seen and possibly rescued by the American forces. It was becoming more obvious to the crew that it was very important, at least to their Chetnik guard, that Chetniks and no one else would rescue this crew. Still, Lt. Grossman and crew kept their attitude towards their Chetnik friends hidden.

## Chapter 9

As the days at the farm languished on with little food and sleeping the nights away on the uncomfortable straw beds on the floor, the men began to itch and scratch as much as their Chetnik friends had been doing all along. It seems they all had a bad case of lice! "I hope these bugs aren't carrying any diseases?" remarked Sgt. Baker. "No, don't worry. With all the shots we had to get when we were shipped out, no disease from this tiny bug is going to get us," said Sgt. White while squeezing the life out of one of the pests between his fingers. For their amusement, the crew would pick out the tiny blood suckers one by one and compare the total of lice each had collected off their scalps. They would also have to shed their clothes and shake them out quite often. The discomfort of the lice was the least of their problems. As January turned to February, the increasingly anxious crew were no closer to rescue then when they first crash landed. Thoughts turned to home and what their worrying loved ones must be going through while waiting for answers.

On February 5th, 1945, in the south Boston neighborhood of Dorchester, it was a clear, cold and breezy Monday afternoon, with snow on the ground from the snowfall a few days earlier. Mrs. Mary Keane was seated in the kitchen of her home on Neponset Avenue talking with her twenty-two-year-old daughter Margaret, the middle of her five children. Margaret had recently married in November of 1944 to a Navy aviation radioman and survivor of the Pearl Harbor attack. The two had met while he was stationed for a couple of months in Boston and began courting before his eventual shipping out to England in preparation for the D-day invasion of Europe.

Mary and her daughter were discussing Margaret's plans for a springtime train trip to visit with her in-laws in Lincoln, Nebraska whom she had yet to meet in person. She would then travel to a U.S. Naval base in Corpus Christie, Texas and join her husband, John, who had been stationed there shortly after returning from overseas. "Mom, I'm a bit nervous about this trip. I've never even met any of Johnny's family. You know he has seven brothers and sisters?" "Oh stop your worrying Marguerite" said Mary. "It's only for a few days, then you'll be off to be with Johnny." "Well, visiting his family in Nebraska is one thing, but what's there to do in Texas? Johnny will be on duty most of the time. I'll just be bored waiting for him to get off duty" said Margaret. "Well, it's only for a few months. You'll be coming back to Boston in the summer right?" responded Mary. "Yes Mother, I suppose I'll manage," said Margaret. Soon, Mary's husband, Thomas Keane Sr. arrived home. Thomas was an Irish immigrant from County Limerick, Ireland. He had just finished his shift as a conductor for the Massachusetts Transit Authority (MTA). He had no sooner sat down to read the paper when the doorbell rang. Thomas rose to see who was at the front door. When he opened the door, he was greeted by a Western Telegram delivery man. "Telegram sir," said the delivery man as he handed Mr. Keane a small envelope and asked for his signature. Mary and Margaret came in from the kitchen and asked Thomas about the telegram he was beginning to open. He pulled out the single page letter and began reading aloud. *"To Mr. and Mrs. Thomas J. Keane Sr. "The Secretary of War desires me to express his deep regret that your son first Lt. Thomas J. Keane Jr. has been reported missing in action since twenty-one January over Yugoslavia…..* "Missing in action? Thomas is missing?" cried out Mary. "How, why…?" "What else does it say, Dad?" Margaret said, her voice trembling with worry over the news about her brother. "It says not much else except that they will notify us if they receive further details or other information" replied Thomas Sr. Margaret began consoling her weeping Mother as she struggled to keep her composure. Meanwhile, Thomas slumped down in his chair, not saying a word as he was shaken by the tragic news that his only son was missing in action. The only thing left for him to do pray. Later that evening, the Keane family went to nearby St. Ambrose Catholic church and lit prayer candles. They would continue to do so until their boy came home safe. This scene typified what many American families of servicemen had to endure during the second world war, including every family member of the crew hiding out at the Cvijanovic's farm in Yugoslavia. While families of MIAs held out hope that their loved ones were safe or perhaps captured at the very least, the not knowing, or not getting any news regarding their welfare with each passing day was surely heart wrenching. Soon after receiving the Western Union telegrams, each of the missing crew's next of kin received letters from Major E.A. Bradunas, Chief of Notification Branch, Personal Affairs Division of the Army Air Forces headquarters in Washington, DC.

The letters offered more details about the last time the crew's B-17 bomber had been seen, which was near the Hungary and Yugoslavian border. The letter let the families of the crew know that as the bomber fell behind the formation, that communication was lost between their plane and the rest of the formation. That fact alone surely left an unsettling feeling for the families of each member of the crew. Did the plane suddenly take a direct hit from flak and blow up killing all on board before a distress call was heard? Were they shot down by German fighters? If so, did any crew member bailout? These were thoughts many of the crew member's families, such as Lt. Keane's, were left pondering with extreme worry. One other bit of information in the letter that each of the crew's families received was that it contained the names and addresses of the next of kin of each crewman. This way, they could write to each other and share their concerns with other family members of the crew. It was a way to unite and bond the mothers and wives of the crew. The same bond the crew themselves formed towards one another, living out their ordeal as MIAs. One of the several letters written was this one written by Sgt. Gourley's mother in Lycan, Colorado to Lt. Keane's mother in Boston:

*"Dear Mrs. Keane, No doubt my letter will be a surprise to you, but my son James R. Gourley has been missing with his crew since Jan. 21, and your son was one of the crew, so I've wondered if you had heard anything more than I have. I got a letter from his commanding officer saying they had made their mission, released their bombs over their target and was returning when their plane began to lose speed and get out of formation in the vicinity of Gyor, Hungary. And was last seen over the Yugoslavia and Hungary line. And I suppose you too got the names of all his crew and relatives addresses. How long had your boy been across? And how many missions had he made? Also, I would like to know his age. My boy had been across since August. He flew across and had made most all of his missions in. He was on his 47th or 48th mission. He is 26 years old. We had been looking forward that he was on his way home when we got the telegram with the tragic news that he was missing. We haven't given up hope as yet. God is the same yesterday, today and forever. And I pray the He will hear and answer our prayers and that our boys will soon return to us. These are very anxious moments. We live in the country, and I can hardly wait for the mail. And then when it comes…no word and I am so disappointed. I would like to hear from you real soon. With much sympathy,*

*A brokenhearted Mother" -Mrs. M.R. Gourley Lycan, Colo.*

Another letter was written in response to Lt. Daniels' mother (Mrs. Isabelle Daniels) in New Rochelle, New York from Sgt. LeClair's mother in Keene, New Hampshire read:

*Dear Mrs. Daniels, Received your nice letter and thanks a lot for writing. I know how you must feel, and our sympathy is with you as there is a lot of us that are going through the same ordeal. We have tried very hard to believe that we will hear that they are alright and have prayed constantly for their safe return.*

*Things are looking a lot better over there, and I don't think it will be very long before we hear some news and pray to God it will be good news. If I hear any news, I will write you immediately and would appreciate it if you did the same.*

*Very sincerely, Mrs. Francis LeClair  -*

Letters like these were commonly written by all the mothers and wives of the crew during the time they were missing in action. Writing letters to each other reminded them that they were not alone in these unsettled, anxious times. They found great comfort in sharing their concerns and sympathy with each other.

Back at the  Cvijanovic's' farm, Mr. Cvijanovic continued his routine of going into town almost daily to gather intelligence for  the crew while they stayed at his farm. One day in mid-February the crew was gathered inside the farmhouse waiting for Mr. Cvijanovic to return from Celinac. Suddenly, Mr. Cvijanovic arrived in a rush and first told the Chetnik escort and then in German, he told Sgt. Taxel that the Germans and Ustachis were close by and it looked like they may be coming up to the farm to search for the missing crew! Sgt. Taxel translated the information to Lt. Grossman and the rest of the crew. Mr. Cvijanovic told the escort and crew to move quickly and go with his son Mico who would lead the crew further up the mountain to a sheep shed that Mr. Cvijanovic had used from time to time. The Chetnik escort, the crew, plus the two B-24 crewmen sprung to life and quickly filed out the front door of the farmhouse and followed Mr. Cvjianovic's teenage son and started running as fast as they could in the snow pack up to the treeline and disappeared into the forest. Mico led the group about a mile up the mountain before they arrived at the sheep shed. It was very cold, and the wooden shed was not insulated and was full of splits in the wood allowing the wind to penetrate the interior. But at least it was a bit of shelter from the cold. There was nothing inside the shed except an empty kettle in a makeshift fireplace that amounted to a hole in the dirt floor they could use to start a fire to melt snow into drinking water. There also was a pile of chopped logs stacked in the corner of the shed. Fortunately most of the crew still had a book of matches, so they could light a fire to keep warm. It seemed as if they would have to hide out through the night and without a fire, they might freeze. Mica left and headed back to the farmhouse. He told the Chetnik that he would return to let them know as soon as his father told him the coast was clear. As night fell, the crew collected some of the wood logs to start a fire. It took a while to get the fire going in the cold temperatures, but eventually Sargents White and Gourley were successful in getting a fire started. The men hunkered down and huddled up as close to the warm fire as possible throughout the cold night. Lt. Grossman, ignoring the Chetnik "guard," ordered the men to take turns getting some sleep so that the fire could stay lit all night. But as it turned out, hardly anyone slept. Shortly after sunrise the next day, Mica arrived and told the men that the coast was clear and that they could return to the farmhouse. When they arrived Mrs. Cvijanovich prepared a breakfast consisting of the same watery porridge made of cornmeal that the crew had become accustomed to and a small piece of gritty cornbread. Both dishes lacked flavor but the men were hungry and would have eaten the porridge and bread if it had been made of sawdust. The Cvijanovics, like many in the neighboring farms, had to ration their food due to the Germans taking most of their summer crops of potatoes, wheat, and corn. And food additives like salt and sugar were worth their weight in gold. Salt was kept in small supply and only used on rare occasions. Salt was used for trade for other needed items between the villagers. Sugar, on the other hand, was practically non-existent in the mountain villages since the Nazi occupation. The men were not getting much to eat, and by now they were showing signs of weight loss. Sgt. Baker began complaining of his stomach bothering him. Soon the others all started experiencing stomach pains, some worse than others. Making matters worse for the crew, the lice problem was not getting any better as they were crawling under the crew's clothing and on to their skin, especially in the thighs and lower back where the itching was hardest to scratch. The crew could at least wash their hands and each day they stayed at the farm. One of the Cvjanovic's daughters would bring in a wooden bucket of snow to melt over the fire, but in winter the only real way to bathe was by way of a damp wash cloth which wasn't much of a wash. Some of the crew began to grumble. "Boy, I could sure use a nice hot bath and a shave," said Sgt. LeClaire. "Yeah, and I never realized how much I miss my toothbrush" added Sgt. White. Lt. Grossman reassured his crew," It could be a lot worse. We could be captured, wasting away in some prison camp, and I'm sure we wouldn't be fed any better."

After some morning chores, Mr. Cvijanovic came in through the front door and greeted the crew before sitting at the table. Sgt. Taxel joined him at the table as Mr. Cvjanovic started speaking to him in German. He expressed his apologies for any inconvenience he may have caused for having the crew spend the night in the sheep shed. He then spoke about what he learned about the German troop movement. Sgt. Taxel then translated to Lt. Grossman and the rest of the crew what Mr. Cvijanovic was telling them. He explained that a column of German soldiers was retreating north and a small patrol of German soldiers had turned east and headed up the mountain trails most likely looking for alternate trails to use to keep off the main routes since the Partisans were closing in. According to some accounts from neighboring farmers, the German patrol was about a quarter of a mile from the Cvijanovic's farm when they suddenly stopped. The patrol turned and headed back down the mountain trail. Most likely, they received a message from a German superior officer to stay on the main routes and engage the Communists if necessary. Once he was sure the area was safe, he sent his son up the mountain in the morning to let the Chetnik escort and the crew know that they could return to the farmhouse. The Partisans were never far off from mountain villagers since the crew had crash landed. The battlefront with the Germans had stalled in the south. But by mid-February, the Partisans fueled by help from the Soviet Army were making advances to the north and closing in on German positions in the valley below. From the Cvijanovic's farm the crew could hear the artillery gunfire in the distance getting closer. As the days went on, the sound of the war seemed to be closing in all around them.

Throughout February, the Chetnik's would send a couple of escorts to the Cvijanovic's farm to gather the crew. Each time the Chetnik escorts would tell the crew that they would be taking them to General Mihailovic's headquarters in Pranjani where allied planes were waiting to transport them back to Italy. However each time the Chetniks would attempt to escort the crew, they would have to abort and bed down at another Chetnik outpost before heading back to the Cvijanovic's farm due to the roads to Pranjani being patrolled by the Germans or Ustachis. Only women and children were allowed to pass through the various checkpoints. Most of the time they traveled on foot during the night since it lowered their chance of getting spotted by the enemy, and as far as the Chetniks were concerned, the Partisans. On one of their failed attempts to reach Mihailovic,s headquarters, the crew came upon a portion of the Vrbajani river. The same river Sargents Taxel and

Sparks had crossed by sleigh when it was frozen. This time there was a small rowboat on the shore they could use. There was only room for three men on this little wooden boat. And to make matters worse, the boat leaked! So the Chetnik escorts took turns rowing two men at a time across the river as quickly and quietly as possible all the while bailing out as much water as possible to avoid sinking into the icy water. Each time one group of men reached the shore on the other side of the river, they would have to bail out water before the escort could row back across to pick up another pair of the crew. Many even chuckled at the absurdity of their predicament with the leaky boat. Each pair of men flailing their arms as they continuously bailed out the water while the escorts were frantically telling the Americans "shhh….Partisans!" Though the crew were secretly praying that the Partisans would find them. But they still could not let on about their hopes to come into contact with the Communists in the presence of the Chetnik escorts. Finally the cold, wet, and weary crew and their escorts found themselves back at the Cvjanoivic's farm once again. Another time they set out to reach Pranjani with another route patrolled this time by the by Ustachi, the exhausted crew had to turn back and eventually spent the night outside using a snow wall to protect them from the wind chill and some broken tree branches to sleep on. That was one of the crews roughest nights. They huddled close together, doing their best to keep warm in the freezing temperatures.

By now the crew was losing patience with the Chetniks. Every attempt at getting to Mihailovic's headquarters was failing. And not only were their promises of a rescue becoming redundant, but the constant,exaggerated dramatization by their Chetnik escorts about the dangers of falling into the hands of the Communist Partisans was getting tiresome. Some fresh escorts were rotating in with the same order to protect the American crew from capture. Most of the Chetnik escorts treated the crew quite well. However the attitude of a couple of the replacement escorts was that of contempt towards the Americans. For example, one of the escorts who joined the group liked to march in the rear of the line on their treks back to the Cvjanovic's. He found great amusement in shooting his rifle over the back of the heads of the crew to watch them hit the ground in momentary fear. He would have a nice laugh at the expense of panicked Americans lying in the snow. An infuriated Lt. Grossman demanded that the escort stop firing his weapon over the heads of his crew.  But the Chetnik would only shrug as if he couldn't understand English. Why this Chetnik escort was behaving inappropriately towards the Americans is a mystery. But a few of the crewmen speculated that this particular Chetnik was one of the many who was angry at the Allies for providing supply drops to the Partisans. Unfortunately, the crew was in no position to challenge the Chetnik's feelings or position regarding when, where and to whom the allies chose to drop supplies. They were in HIS homeland now, and the thought was that doing anything to cause friction would do more harm than good. But while the crew was thankful that they were not held captive and were generally treated well, the gun-play of the Chetnik guard was causing some resentment to surface within the crew. One day as a few of the crew were outside milling about the farm waiting for Mr. Cvijanovic to return from his intelligence gathering trip to town, another Chetnik soldier was talking to the men in broken but understandable English. He said, "You Amerikanos are very lucky to be alive. If you did not have us to protect you, surely you would not make it. After we help you get back to Italia, I hope your government pays us well for keeping you out of the hands of your enemy. You know the Germans? They pay for Amerikanos." He seemed to be threatening the Americans. It did not go unnoticed by any of the crew. A few of the crew were annoyed at the Chetnik's bravado. He went on. "Your country stopped sending supplies and instead supplies our Partisan enemies. We fight the Germans. Where is your army? You drop bombs, but are afraid to fight on the ground with us?" Sgt. White had heard enough of the Chetnik's rant. He spoke up. "We're not afraid to fight. You think flying bombing missions are easy?" The Chetnik began provoking a few of the crew. "OK, let's see how strong and brave Amerikano is. Anyone of you cares to wrestle with me?" he asked. Without missing a beat Sgt. White, who was known for never backing down to a challenge said, "I will, right now!" The Chetnik soldier leaned his rifle against the tool shed and the men both started going at it! The Chetnik was about the same build and height as Sgt. White which was about five feet, ten inches, and about one hundred and fifty pounds. As the men were wrestling and rolling on the ground, the rest of the crew began cheering on Sgt. White. For the time being all the action seemed to be in fun, much in the same way brothers might wrestle with each other. But then the Chetnik started turning more aggressive. Sgt. White had by this time had enough and quickly turned over the top of the Chetnik and pinned him to the ground before Lt.s Grossman and Daniels came running out of the farmhouse after hearing the ruckus and broke it up. Though no punches were thrown and neither man hurt, (except perhaps the Chetnik soldier's pride having been pinned in the dirt) the Chetniks never again challenged any of the crew to a wrestling match. The rest of the crew tried to downplay it to avoid troubling the embarrassed Chetnik, but every member of the crew gave Sgt White the "atta boy" treatment after the Chetnik brushed himself off and returned to his post near the entrance of the farm. And for a while this little skirmish bolstered the morale of the crew. So much so that Lt. Grossman never gave Sgt White any reprimand. He did however tell the crew that they best avoid any confrontations with the Chetniks in the future.

## Chapter 10

One chilly afternoon Mr. Cvijanovic came in from doing some chores with his sons and had the men sit at the table. He noticed Sargents Baker and Gourley were having stomach problems far worse than usual. He poured them each a full glass of Rakija (a strong plum brandy) and said in English "bottoms up!" Sgt. Baker couldn't drink more than a sip because he was feeling pretty nauseous, but Sgt. Gourley drank the whole glass in one large gulp. After a while he said with a bit of a slur "hey, my bellyache is gone." Of course he found it difficult to walk a straight line for a while, but at least he felt better. Perhaps the alcohol killed off the bacteria from the rotted goat meat in his gut. Everyone suffered from stomach problems. Some of the crew were worse off than others. A good swig of Rakija became the crew's medicine.

Meanwhile, Sgt. Taxel had become quite friendly with Mr. Cvjanovic. Their budding friendship was buoyed by the fact that they could speak a common (German) language. Sgt. Taxel began to learn more and more about the Serbian people. Their customs, religion, politics and he was quite taken with the old farmer and his family. He was impressed with the closeness, love, respect and loyalty the Cvijanovic family displayed towards each other and how Mr. and Mrs. Cvijanovic seemed to care for the welfare of the crew as if they were their own sons. Sgt. Taxel turn would tell Mr. Cvijanovic all about America. In particular, his hometown of Brooklyn, New York. During one of their conversations Mr. Cvijanovic offered Sgt. Taxel and each crew member a piece of his several acres of land after the war if they wanted to stay in Yugoslavia. Sgt. Taxel translated Mr. Cvijanovic's generous offer to all of the crew. Of course each of the crew members thanked Mr. Cvijanovic, but politely declined. They couldn't wait to get back to the U.S.A. At one point during their many conversations, Sgt. Taxel made a special promise to Mr. Cvijanovich. He promised that if they made it back to America, he would make arrangements to sponsor his youngest son, Momchilo ("Mo") to come live with him in New York when the ten year-old became of legal age. With the unsure stability of the future of Yugoslavia, Mr. Cvijanovic accepted Sgt. Taxel's promise. Mr. Cvijanovic was thrilled with the possibility of his son going to America in the future. A country he knew very little about except how much more wealthy the Americans were. Mr. Cvijanovic loved and cared for each of his children. And he would hate being separated from any of them. But he knew that if any of his children had the opportunity to live in America it would mean the chance of a much better life. Better than a life spent in a post-war Yugoslavia. The country was looking more likely that it would fall into Tito's Communist regime by wars end.

As February came to an end, the beginning of March found the weather turning slightly warmer but it still had the bite of winter's chill. The American bomber crew was still nowhere close to being evacuated back to their base at Sterparone. True they were safe at Mr. Cvjanovic's farm for the time being,but fear of capture was always permeating among the crew. As leader of the crew Lt. Grossman had by now nearly lost all faith in the Chetnik's chances of rescue despite their continued promises. In fact the entire crew's impatience with the Chetniks was becoming the main topic of discussion among themselves. Every attempt at evacuation failed, and they would eventually be forced to return to the Cvijanovics farm to avoid the enemy. When Mr. Cvijanovic would return from the nearby towns and villages with the daily intelligence report, it was always the same bad news regarding the safety of using the main roads and trails to Pranjani. While Lt. Grossman and the rest of the crew were very grateful to the Cvijanovics for risking their lives to hide them at their farm, the Americans were nearing the breaking point regarding the Chetnik soldiers ability to help get them out of Yugoslavia. In short,the evacuation plan had to change. The talks between the crew began to lean heavily on taking their chances and seeking out the Partisans on their own if necessary. At first Sgt. Taxel argued against that move. He preferred to wait it out at the farm until it was determined safe to move out. He believed that the Germans and Ustachis would soon be out of the territory with the advancements being made by the Communist armies.  But Lt. Grossman and the rest of the crew wouldn't be alone in their decision to take their chances and seek out the Partisans sooner than wait out the tides of war. Sgt. Taxel soon came to agree with his fellow crew members when  Mr. Cvijanovic finally came forth and voiced his agreement to the airmen that a new plan was needed. However, it was a decision that was most difficult for him to conclude. Mr. Cvijanovic had very much wanted the Chetniks to be the group that would guide the American flyers to their eventual rescue. The Chetniks were his people. The Partisans were mostly made up of communist sympathizers who he believed would destroy his freedom and way of life in the country. But the Partisans were fighting the Germans in large numbers and the

Chetnik resistance was becoming weaker. It was apparent to the farmer that it was time for the crew to abandon the good intentions of the Chetniks. In reality Mr. Cvijanovic knew this deep down for some time. He knew ever since Lt. Grossman broached the subject of receiving help from the Partisans not long after he took the crew in at his farm. But he had always balked at the idea of letting them go off to the Partisans. After all he would be risking his relationships with his Chetnik compatriots if word got out that he helped deliver the fugitive American crew to the Chetnik's most despised enemy. Another reason he stayed mum on the subject of a Partisan led rescue for so long was that he was afraid if he told them where they could reach the Partisan camp the crew might leave his farm in haste putting the crew at risk of capture by the Germans or Ustachi before reaching the Partisans. But more importantly he was extremely fond of the American crew and sincerely wanted what was best for them to stay alive. Yet morally he felt it would be wrong to allow the Chetnik guards to continue escorting the crew, going in circles trying and failing each time to get through to Mihailovic's headquarters, taking essentially the same risk as it would for the crew to seek out a Partisan camp.

So Mr. Cvijanovic approached Sgt. Taxel and started speaking to him. Sgt. Taxel then found Lt. Grossman and asked him to gather the rest of the crew at the table inside the farmhouse. With Sgt. Taxel translating, Mr. Cvijanovivc spoke. "The only way for you to get out of the country is to go to the Partisans. The Chetniks cannot get you out of the country. I spoke to some villagers in Celinac. They told me that Tito's Partisans are advancing on German positions from the south and are pushing north. I heard that some Chetniks are joining the Germans fight against Partisans. I think you will be better off going with the Partisans" he said. Of course Lt. Grossman had already come to that conclusion privately in discussions among his crew earlier. But to hear Mr. Cvijanovic finally speak in agreement meant he would have his much needed help in getting to the Partisans. Back in January, when the Americans first arrived at his farm, Mr. Cvijanovic had hoped the crew would be able to stay until perhaps the war ended with the hope that the anticipated Western Allies landing would keep the country from falling into the hands of the Communists. But deep down he knew he couldn't keep the crew at his home for much longer, especially with the  Communists advancing closer each day.  He was also well aware that his American friends who he called "his sons" must have families back in America that were sick with worry over their missing loved ones.

Lt. Grossman and the crew knew they would need a plan to get to the Partisan side. But with two Chetnik guards watching over them at all times it might be difficult. It's not that the guards were a serious threat, but if they were to find out about the American's intentions to find the Partisans they might report it their superiors who would be forced to stop them in their tracks. Usually two Chetnik soldiers took turns standing watch outside the farmhouse occasionally peering through the window near the front door to peek at the sleeping crew. While one guard kept watch the other would retire to one of the sheds on the property and get a couple of hours of sleep. One evening Lt. Grossman and Sgt. Taxel summoned Mr. Cvijanovic, and the three of them came up with a plan to abandon the aid of the Chetniks and reach the Partisans. Lt. Grossman then consulted with the crew's three other officers Escardo, Keane and Daniels to get their thoughts before filling in the rest of the crew. Despite the risk the plan met with unanimous approval. Mr. Cvijanovic told Lt. Grossman and Sgt. Taxel that he knew some trails that would lead the crew in the general direction of the Partisans' front line about twenty-five miles to the southeast of the farm near the town of Teslic. About fifteen miles further south of Teslic was the village of Zepec (Zepce)located in a valley. The hope was that Zepce was now held by the Partisans. If the crew were able to abandon the Chetnik escorts near Zepec, they might have a chance to make contact with the Partisans. The crew would have to "ditch" the escorts somewhere along the mountain trail and try and make it to that town or any nearby villages and suss out Partisan soldiers or sympathizers. Between Teslic and Zepce located in the valley, up in the mountains above the two towns there was a Chetnik outpost in an empty hunting shed that would serve ostensibly as a relay point before turning east towards Pranjani. The crew would have to stay on the trail that was in the mountains that followed along a ridge along the Danaric Alps to avoid enemy detection. At various points, connecting trails winded down to the valley below where the Partisans were engaging the Germans. Fortunately with the Partisans advancement in the south moving north, Mr. Cvjijanovic's daily intelligence reports indicated that most of the Germans were retreating from the south keeping to the valleys below where the roads could accommodate the large contingent of soldiers and equipment retreating northwest. However parts of the trail were still in Ustachi territory so they would have to be very careful. Since a few of the crew including Sgt. Baker were still armed with their .45 caliber pistols, they felt it gave them at least a small fighting chance should they run into a retreating German or Ustachi patrol. All in all it was worth the risk as far as they were concerned. Mr.

Cvijanovic could not lead the crew himself to the Partisans because the repercussions would cause him great trouble if he were seen turning allied airmen over to a company of Partisan armed fighters.

So the plan's objective was for the crew to reach the Partisans to the southeast, but without the Chetnik's knowledge beforehand. For starters, Mr. Cvijanovic had to convince the two guards that he had gathered some new intelligence that might help in guiding the American crew to General Mihailovic's headquarters without a high risk of detection from the Ustachis,Germans or even the Partisans. The next day Mr. Cvijanovic spoke to the Chetnik guards and began telling them that the eastbound trails near the town of Teslic that they had used to attempt to transport the crew to Pranjani failed because they had always run into German or Ustachi patrols forcing them to return. Then Mr. Cvijanovich suggested the alternate southeast bound route towards the town of Zepce further south. He explained that it would have to be a much longer journey, and as usual, they must travel in the protection of darkness during the night mostly on foot. Mr. Cvijanovic ostensibly explained to the Chetnik soldiers that using an alternate trail in the mountains located just north of Zepce would lead them to Pranjani. It would take several days, but it would be the best chance to get them through. Later that evening one of the guards left the farm to report what Mr. Cvijanovic suggested about the safe route to take the Americans on to Pranjani. The Chetniks had no reason to doubt the old man since they were quite aware of his knowledge of the area and his reputation among many Chetnik leaders. The following day, the Chetnik guard returned with another Chetnik soldier. This Chetnik looked younger,barely out of high school. After speaking privately with the young Chetnik for a while, Mr. Cvijanovic approached the crew who were off in the distance careful not to arouse suspicion from the guard. He then told Sgt. Taxel who translated to Lt. Grossman and the rest of the crew that the Chetnik soldiers took the bait. The plan was on.

The Chetniks would make preparations to move them out yet again. Only this time Lt. Grossman and crew were determined not to return to the Cvijanovich's farm. They had put the family at risk enough and everyone was anxious to try and make it to the coastal region. Mr. Cvijanovich told the crew that the Chetniks informed him that they would have two escorts depart with the crew on Thursday, March 9th. They would leave the Cvijanovic farm during the evening hours to avoid possible detection by neighboring farmers who might be on the take for the Germans. Mr. Cvijanovich went to great lengths to not only hide the crew from the Germans and

Ustachis, but he was careful never to mention the Americans to anyone in the farm community. It was not that he didn't trust his neighbors, it was for their protection. The less his friends knew the better off they would be in case they were ever interrogated. But it was always a possibility that any one of the Chetnik escorts might act carelessly. A single Chetnik could divulge the American's connection with Mr. Cvijanovich while in the company of other farmers in the area. There might be serious consequence should any of the Cvijanovic's neighbors succumb to interrogation by either the Germans or the Partisans and be forced to inform on the Cvijanovic family.

Two days before the crew's planned departure, a Chetnik soldier brought a young man to hide out at the Cvijanovic's farmhouse. Mr. Cvijanonvic welcomed the man into his house. Many of the crew thought to themselves sarcastically, this was all they needed, another person to worry about. The man was an Italian dressed in civilian clothes. Mr. Cvijanovic and also Lt. Escardo spoke to the young man since he too was familiar with the Italian language. It wasn't long before Lt. Grossman, and the crew learned he could be trusted. The man claimed he was not a loyal fascist. He told Lt. Escardo that he had been in the Italian Army at the start of the occupation of Yugoslavia but only because he had no choice. Lt. Escardo translated into English that the young man told him he had been looking for help getting back to his homeland ever since the Italians had changed sides from the Axis to the Allies. He had ditched his uniform for civilian clothes and headed up to the mountains where it was safe. He could speak the language of the locals since he used to travel often with his family as a boy to Yugoslavia before the war so that he could blend in with the mountain population. He spent over a year drifting from one farm to another working for food and shelter and keeping out of sight from the Germans or Ustachi. He said he learned who Mr. Cvijanovic was from another farmer who helped him make contact with the Chetniks and that convinced the Chetniks that he was not an enemy of the Serbs and could be trusted in Mr. Cvjanovic's care for the time being. He was afraid that if the Germans or Ustachi found him first, he would be shot as a traitor if his nationality were to be discovered. It put him in the same predicament as the American airmen. (As a footnote: No one in the crew could remember the Italian civilian's name).

After settling in, Lt. Escardo briefed the Italian about their plan on leaving for the Partisans. They had no choice but to trust that he could keep their plan a secret from the Chetniks. Of course he too wanted to leave Yugoslavia for Italy, so he was only too happy to go along with American's plan. Lt. Escardo argued he could be useful to the crew once they freed themselves from the Chetnik escorts since he spoke Slavic. With everyone briefed and the Chetnik outpost prepared, all that was left to do for now was to get some rest before the long trek. The days leading up to their departure of the farm were spent laying low, relaxing and not only thinking about home and their loved ones which daily consumed their thoughts, but also of their squadron mates and how they were faring on the continued bombing campaign.

Back at the air base in Sterparone, the crew's squadron commanding officer, Major Leo C. Brooks was holding out hope that Lt. Grossman and his crew were alive and among friendlies. He knew only too well what it felt like to be missing in action. Major Brooks himself was flying as a substitute co-pilot on July 15th, 1944 and was shot down after getting hit by flak on a mission to bomb the oil refineries at Ploesti. He and his crew bailed out over eastern Yugoslavia about 20 miles northeast of the town of Nis in what is now Serbia. He was immediately rescued by Chetniks who walked he and his crew over several days through mountainous terrain the ninety plus miles to Mihailovic's headquarters in Pranjani. Then a Captain and West Point grad, Brooks joined several other downed allied airmen at Pranjani who were aided by Chetniks. Since he was the ranking officer among the evaders, he took command and helped plan the evacuation that later became known as "Operation Halyard." Using the former British liaison airfield at Pranjani near General Mihailovic's Chetnik headquarters, Captain Brooks used Mihailovic's radio to make contact with the 15th Air Force Headquarters in Italy. He used a code the downed American airmen had devised to prevent the Germans from intercepting the message. Captain Brooks organized adding length to the runway since it was too short for the C-47 transport planes. Then on the evening of August 9th, 1944, four C-47's landed one by one at Pranjani. Using runners and Chetnik soldiers to help load the injured and sick airmen on to the first plane, the next plane would land and take on more men. The men were dispersed in the woods bordering the airstrip and would come out in small groups of three or four men at a time and board the transport when signaled. Each plane could take only about twenty men at a time. Ninety-six downed airmen made it on to the C-47's and flew safely back to Italy that evening. But the evacuation had to pause until the next morning due to a lack of available transport aircraft. The next morning on August 10th, the first of many C-47's landed at Pranjani. Plane after plane arrived to pick up more airmen.

The Chetniks set up a large perimeter around the airfield to fend off any possible German ground attack while P-51 Mustang fighters flown by the Tuskegee Airmen of the 332$^{nd}$ Fighter Group based at Cattolica, Italy flew cover over the field and escorted the transport planes to and from Pranjani. Captain Brooks was the last man on the last plane that took off and headed back to Italy. A total of two hundred and forty allied airmen, mostly Americans, were airlifted to safety that day. Many more evacuations were planned during August of 1944. Major Brooks later told many of his squadron comrades that without the help of the Tuskegee Airmen, the Chetnik soldiers and the local Serbian population, the operation would have failed. For his efforts in Operation Halyard, Captain Brooks was awarded the Distinguished Flying Cross, was promoted to Major and was designated as commander of the 840$^{th}$ squadron of the 483$^{rd}$ bomb group. Major Brooks fared much better with the Chetnik's aid than Lt. Grossman and crew. But had he parachuted over Banja Luca and landed near the site when and where Lt. Grossman's crew crash landed, he most certainly would not have been airlifted out of Yugoslavia, no matter how much help the Chetniks could render.

However hopeful he was, Major Brooks feared that Lt. Grossman and crew went down in a more Nazi occupied territory in Yugoslavia based on eyewitness reports that claimed the plane was last seen heading southwest over the borders of Hungary and Yugoslavia. It had been several weeks since Lt. Grossman's plane went missing and if they had made it to friendly territories in Hungary, he most certainly would have received word by now. And since there was no word from the Red Cross to report that they were captured and taken prisoners by the Germans, it left Major Brooks with two possible scenarios. One is that they were rescued and held by Partisans until they could turn them over to Russian forces coming in from the north and east of Yugoslavia or the second scenario in which they had been killed in action. As squadron commander, killed, wounded and missing air crews weighed heavily on his mind. Knowing that the Partisans were also advancing on German-held positions in Yugoslavia, Major Brooks began to think that no matter how much the Chetniks wanted to help them, a rescue by Partisans was the crew's best chance in getting evacuated back to Italy. Little did he know just how accurate he was in that thinking.

## Chapter 11

As March 9th turned into evening, Mrs. Cvijanovic started preparing a meal of cornmeal porridge for her family but made sure all the Americans were served first. Mr. Cvijanoivic went out to the nearby shed and invited the two Chetniks to join them in the house if they were hungry and wanted to grab a bite to eat before heading out. One of the Chetnik escorts, the older of the two, spoke a little English. While this made communicating with him easier Lt. Grossman reminded his crew to be careful not to speak about their intentions within earshot.  After dinner each of the crew quietly thanked Mr. And Mrs.Cvijanovic for all they had done to help them evade capture and for feeding them and letting them hide out. Then the crew said goodbye to their six children. The youngest child Momchilo was especially sad to see the Americans leave. He was very fond of his "big American brothers" and was going to miss them terribly. He had witnessed the crew leaving his house many times before with the Chetnik escorts, but they always ended up back at his Father's house. However this time he knew it was most likely goodbye for good. His Father had prepared the youngster and his siblings that he was sure the Americans would not be returning this time. Momchilo began to cheer up when he remembered Sgt. Taxel's promise to help him come to America when he got older. As the crew filed outside with the two Chetnik escorts, Sgt. Taxel was the last to say goodbye to Mr. and Mrs. Cvijanovic. Speaking in German, the two exchanged kind words of thanks and appreciation and reaffirming his promise he made regarding his youngest son while firmly shaking hands. Then in his native Serbian language Mr. Cvijanovic said, "Zbogom  sine moj" ("goodbye my sons") and Sgt. Taxel joined the others out in front of the house. Then the crew marched off down the road into the night, nervously hoping that their plan to separate from the "aid"of the Chetniks would work and that they would soon be in the hands of the Partisans and eventually get back to Foggia.

About a mile away, at the bottom of the road that led the crew from the Cvijanovic's farm, two horse driven sleighs were waiting for them as arranged by the Chetniks the day before. They all climbed aboard crowding six men into one sleigh and seven in the other and off they went. They traveled the first part of the journey, north towards Banja Luca. Lt. Keane had a small compass in his pocket and took it out along with a tiny pencil and notepaper he had with him. He started mapping the crew's travels for a keepsake. Looking at his compass, it showed that they were indeed traveling north. "I hope these Chetniks know where they're going ?" said Lt. Keane. "Yeah, I hope we don't run into any Germans." replied Lt. Daniels. "Tell me again, why are we heading towards Banja Luca?" he asked. "We must go this way because we have to use the bridge. This is the only way to cross the river" said the Chetnik seated in their sleigh. "Oh I see" Lt. Daniels replied, sounding a bit embarrassed. They had to cross two small bridges at separate locations over the Vrbanja River. The river snaked into two large bends shaped like a backward "S." One bend was just south of Celinac and the other bend to the north side of the town. A tributary of the larger Vrbas River, the Vrbanja River's winter ice had broken up making it impossible for the sleighs to cross the river without using the bridges. This detour added several hours to their journey, but they had no choice. They also had to avoid going through Celinac with the Germans and Ustachis still present. After crossing the river's bridges, they continued north on the east side of the river. Keeping off the main road from Celinac to Banja Luca, the party turned and headed east a couple of miles south of the entrance to Banja Luca. Then they veered southeast continuing by sleigh until they arrived at the base of the mountain range that was part of the Dinaric Alps, which stretches all along the Adriatic coast from Slovenia to Montenegro and moves inland as wide as one hundred and fifty miles. The sleighs plowed on until they reached the base of the hillside and came to a stop. A couple of Chetniks came out from behind some trees and retrieved the sleighs after the crew was ordered to dismount. "We must walk now" said the Chetnik who had been leading the sleighs. The crew's hope for a long journey by sleigh were dashed. They hiked up to the mountain trail that would take them southeast towards Zepce, bypassing the town Teslic, which is northwest of Zepce. The weather was still cold, especially at night, but by now the freezing winter weather was making way for spring. Snow still covered most of the terrain, but most of the heavier used trails were becoming patches of slush and the thawing ground turning to mud. It became much harder for the crew to hike through mud than it was marching in the snow. Those who were walking in their flight boots, like Sgt. Gourley and Sgt. Baker had a tougher time with aching feet than the others, although the fear of trench foot was on everyone's mind. An even bigger concern was the crew's physical strength which was waning due to the malnutrition each man was experiencing. The Cvijanovics fed them just enough to stay alive, but everyone still hungered. The crew pushed on throughout the night. They came upon a farmer's field and dug up some garlic cloves that were not ready for harvest. But being so hungry for nearly fifty days, they considered anything edible was fair game. Sgt. Gourley had kept a cob of field corn in his flight jacket pocket. He received it back at the Cvijanovic's farm and would take a small nibble to chew on daily. Compared to the bitter taste of unripened garlic, the bland field corn tasted much better. The crew kept walking through the mountains all through the night for several miles taking periodic rests. Later that morning on March 10th, they reached the ridge that stretched along a small section of the mountain range. They were only at about 1,500 feet elevation but without much food to eat it felt like 10,000 feet to the exhausted men. They rested until later in the evening. As tired as they were, they were still a long way from their planned "escape" from the Chetniks.  After spending the afternoon resting, at sunset the crew prepared for the next leg of their journey. In the darkness of nightfall the Chetniks and the crew started out again continuing east towards Teslic, but keeping to the north of the town. At times Lt. Grossman thought about him and the crew deserting the escorts and trying to reach any Partisan sympathizers that might be near Teslic before the Chetniks could overtake them. But he decided it would be too risky to take off with such a long distance yet to walk. Back at his farm a few days earlier Mr. Cvijanovic had convinced the Chetnik escorts that instead of continuing east from Teslic towards Mihailovic's headquarters in Pranjani, like they had tried and failed many times before, that from the proximity of Teslic they should travel several miles south until they reached the eastern outskirts of Zepec. From there they could turn east and head toward Pranjani. The Chetniks had arranged for another escort contingent to meet them there nearby up in the mountains where they would relieve the crew's escorts and take over leading the airmen on the long journey to Pranjani. This detour had been suggested to avoid a heavier concentration of Ustachi sentries still posted on the route east of Banja Luca. And by staying in the mountain trails, the Chetnik escorts believed they could avoid the Partisan soldiers fighting the Germans in the southern valleys. The trail chosen was seldom used except for the occasional hunter because of its rough terrain. But it offered a clear pathway to Pranjani making the plan plausible. Little did the Chetniks know that the crew had no intention of continuing eastbound when they neared Zepec.

The men marched along the mountain trail for what seemed an eternity. Sgt. Baker's feet blistered making it more difficult for him to walk. Others in the crew were suffering from various foot ailments and stomach ailments. Lt. Escardo and

Sgt. Taxel were having a hard time with stomach pains from both the lack of food and the spoiled goat meat they had on occasion back at the farm. Regardless of their ailments, they marched on through the night keeping their thoughts on getting back home for inspiration. Finally just before dawn on March 11th, they completed the long second leg of their journey. They came upon an empty structure resembling a hunting shed nearly twenty miles from their starting point at the farm. The shed was in the mountains a couple of miles past Teslic. After skirting around the fairly large town located in the valley below, they found the empty shed. Exhausted and hungry, this is where they could rest until nightfall before continuing ahead. The crew knew they were getting closer to the Partisans front line. In the distance they could hear the gunfire and artillery cannons the Germans and Partisans were firing at each other. The artillery fire kept the Chetnik escorts on edge. They didn't seem to fear the Germans as much, but the escorts kept making it clear with more of their propaganda that the Partisans would only bring harm to the Americans. In fact it is quite possible that had the crew been stopped by a German patrol, the escorts might have acted as the crew's captors instead of rescuers and collected the three cents in pay for each American airmen as promised by the German command in Yugoslavia.

Lt. Grossman and the crew began conversing out of earshot from the Chetnik escorts who took turns standing watch, especially the escort who understood a bit of English. "I believe we're close to the Partisans just as Mr. Cvijanovic predicted" said Lt. Grossman. "We need a diversion. Any suggestions?" Sgt. Taxel spoke up. "Sgt. Baker's not looking too well Lieutenant. His feet are covered in sores." Lt. Grossman took a look at Sgt. Baker. "Baker, how are your feet doing?" "Not great Lieutenant, but I can still walk" replied Sgt. Baker. "Well do you think you could put up a fuss about not walking any further that will convince one of our Chetnik friends to go for some help?" "Sure Lieutenant, and it won't be much of a stretch of the truth. My feet ARE killing me!" he said. "OK, Baker" replied Lt. Grossman. "If we can get one of these Chetniks to go back for medical supplies, that will leave us with only one guard for the thirteen of us" he added. Lt. Grossman quietly continued conversing with his crew while the two Chetniks were talking among themselves out of earshot, seemingly unconcerned with the Americans. Lt. Grossman approached the Chetnik who understood English and asked that they stay at the shed until the following evening to give his men longer time to recover from walking several miles. The Chetniks agreed to the Lieutenant request to rest until the following evening. The delay would allow the crew to carry out their plan in the morning because as much as broad daylight was risky, they feared more getting lost in the darkness and losing their way. They would be on their own and without the escorts so it was better to see where approximately they were going. Lt. Grossman told the crew, "We'll start off in the morning. If the Chetniks take the bait and one of them goes for help for Baker, we'll split up into two groups. We'll take off in opposite directions. That will cause some confusion among the one Chetnik left watching us. He can only draw his weapon at one group right? As group number one takes off in one direction, group number two will take off in the opposite direction. Whichever group or if both groups get away, we should follow the sound of the artillery fire south of here and try to make contact with the Partisans." "What if the guard fires at us" asked Lt. Daniels. "I don't believe he will, Sandy" replied Lt. Grossman. "They know they have orders not to harm us. We'll just have to trust that they follow those orders." "Lieutenant, why don't we just tell them what we're planning to do?" asked Sgt. White. "They act like they don't care what we do. Neither of these soldiers follows any of us to the bushes when nature calls" he continued. "Well Sargent, if we tell them our plans to find the Partisans, we can't be sure how they'll react" replied Lt. Grossman. The airmen concluded that at best, the remaining guard would panic and run for help allowing both groups to get away. At worst the crew might have to draw their sidearms against the Chetnik escort if he were to try to stop them, holding him at bay then make a run for it. The former scenario was what the crew was hoping would happen. They figured that since they were not prisoners the Chetnik escorts would be in serious trouble if they tried to harm the crew. They only had orders to deliver the crew safely to a relay point near Zepec (Zepce). Fortunately for the crew these two escorts who were guiding them were not as troublesome as some other Chetnik escorts that had guided them, like for instance the soldiers who would fire their guns over the heads of the crew as a cruel joke. Lt. Grossman assigned the crew into the two groups. Each group would be led by two of the crew's officers. Group number one was led by Lieutenants Grossman and Daniels and consisted of Sargents LeClair, Taxel, Baker, and Whetstone of the B-24 crew. Group number two was led by Lt. Escardo and Lt. Keane and consisted of Sargents Gourley, Sparks, White, and Cpl. Howe (the other B-24 crewman), and the Italian civilian. Wrapping up their little meeting in the shed, Lt. Grossman said, "Remember, if any of us are successful at getting away, stay off the main trails as much as possible and head south towards the battlefront. But make sure to keep out of sight until you are positive you've reached the Partisan line. Or if we are lucky, we might make it to the town of Zepec and find some help locating a Partisan camp from the villagers. But try and avoid any contact with Chetnik soldiers. They may mean well, but as Mr. Cvijanovich told us, they can't get us out of the country." The plan had no guarantee to work but every one of the crew agreed it was worth the risk. After a bit more discussion, the tired crew retired for the night.

The next morning on March 12th, after the crew woke up, Sgt. Baker with his stomach ailment and hurting feet tried standing. Acting sicker than he actually was, he suddenly collapsed which alerted the Chetnik escorts to check on his condition. Lt. Grossman insisted to the Chetnik guard who could understand him that he needed to go for help and see if he could bring back some medical supplies for Sgt. Baker's feet and stomach aches. "He can't walk, you need to go get help before we head out tonight. He'll never be able to make it to Pranjani" said Lt. Grossman. After pausing for a minute or two the Chetnik remembered a family back near Teslic that had helped injured Chetnik soldiers before. He then conferred with his comrade and who then quickly took off for help. "He will send for help. He will return before nightfall. We will be safe as long as we wait here in the mountains." said the remaining Chetnik escort. After an hour or two the crew felt the Chetnik who went for help was long gone. So they stood up and formed into two groups as planned. The lone escort was startled and asked what they were doing? Demanding an answer, he then pointed his weapon at them which surprised the crew. Instead of running as they had planned, both groups just froze. Again the Chetnik asked,"Where are you going?" "We are leaving on our own" replied Lt. Grossman. "You are welcome to come with us," said Lt. Escardo. To the crew's amazement, the Chetnik lowered his weapon and told the crew he could not go with them because he would be shot as a traitor if he led them to the Partisans. He also said he would not stop them either. But he told them he would have to go for help and try and "recapture" them later so his superiors wouldn't suspect he just let them go without any protest. Sticking to the plan Lt. Grossman thought they should remain divided into the two groups heading in different directions. Being split up would attract less attention and they could cover more ground increasing their chances of reaching the Partisans. The group led by Lieutenant's Escardo and Keane would stay in the high country heading southeast. They planned on staying on the mountain trails before descending into the valley after they made sure it was safe. Meanwhile the other group led by Lieutenant's Grossman and Daniels would head south along the mountain ridge overlooking the valley below towards Zepce. Both groups would follow the sounds of the artillery in the distance. From the ridge, they could survey the battlefront and stay relatively hidden in the treeline trying to locate the Partisan side before moving towards the valley below. They hoped the valley was not occupied by any retreating Germans. So without resistance from their escort, the two groups began walking, and the Chetnik walked back towards Teslic to catch up to his comrade. If both groups were successful at making contact with the Partisans, they hoped to reunite later with their help. Lt. Grossman wished Escardo and Keane good luck and reminded them to keep the sound of the artillery fire within earshot and keep a lookout for any retreating Germans. The two groups of Americans then went off in separate directions as planned.

## Chapter 12

Lt. Escardo and Lt. Keane's group headed down the trail. They decided that they would scout ahead on the trail so they could avoid the enemy. Escardo and Keane each took turns heading out ahead with another crew member while the rest of their group stayed behind. When each detail had returned from their scouting mission, the group would continue moving on. At one point on a scouting mission Lt. Escardo and Cpl. Howe located a small group of five or six soldiers about a hundred yards ahead sitting off to the side of the trail smoking cigarettes. Not knowing for sure if they were friendly or not, both men quietly retreated to their group and reported what they saw to Lt. Keane and the rest of the group. "You think they are Germans or Ustachis?" asked Lt. Keane. "No, I think they might be Russians" replied Lt. Escardo. If they were indeed Russians, they thought they'd be home free. Lt. Keane opted that they should risk it and continue down the trail. Everyone was tired, hungry, with sore feet and suffering from various stages of stomach disorders. No one objected to going on for at least a closer look. So cautiously they moved on. Sgt. Gourley missed having his sidearm as they marched down the trail. The others who still had their pistols loaded their ammo clips just in case. After walking for about a mile, the group came within sight of the soldiers. The crew had to be sure they were friendlies and not a group of Yugoslavian conscripts fighting on the German side. As the crew crouched in the brush off to the side of the trail, they could see the soldiers talking among themselves. "You're right Escardo, those look like Russian uniforms to me!" exclaimed Lt. Keane. "Let's see if they'll help us Lieutenant!" said Sgt. White. As the American airmen gathered themselves and came out of the brush, rejoining the trail, they then approached the soldiers. Lt. Escardo attempted a simple greeting. But before he could think of a Russian word for "hello" the soldiers quickly stood up and glanced at the crew. With a look of indifference, the soldiers marched a fast-paced walk down the trail leaving behind the bewildered airmen. It was as if the American's interrupted a private gathering and were not welcome to join them. Perhaps the crew stumbled on this particular group of Russian soldiers who were supposed to be at the front or on patrol, but against orders were sneaking a little break in the war. But it was quite certain that these soldiers wanted nothing to do with the American evaders. With the Russian soldiers heading off a few hundred paces ahead of the Americans, Lt. Keane said, "Come on, let's follow them. Maybe they will lead us to their camp?" The group decided to follow along keeping their distance to avoid possibly irritating the soldiers into thinking they were chasing them. After an hour or so, the trail became windier than usual and eventually after coming around a bend, the fast-moving Russians were gone from sight. "Where'd they go?" asked Sgt. Sparks. "Did they just leave the trail?" he added. "Let's stay on this trail. It still might lead us to their camp" said Lt. Escardo.

They finally reached the valley by mid afternoon. The sound of the artillery was getting louder. The battlefront seemed to be closing in. While they hoped they would soon be in the care of friendly forces, they also feared getting captured by German or Ustachi who were in retreat. If capture were to happen, they resisted thinking of the most certain execution they'd face.

They came upon a small town entering from the west. "This must be Zepec" said Lt. Keane. "Are you sure?" asked Lt. Escardo. "Well based on my little compass and Mr. Cvijanovic's general direction, it has to be" Lt. Keane added. Most of the trails were unmarked, and without using a map, it wouldn't be until you were entering a town from the main road that you would know what town you were in. As the men walked through the town, it seemed deserted. But every once in a while as they passed a house they could see the eyes of villagers peeking from behind their curtains. It gave everyone an eerie feeling being watched. They were praying that these folks were not sympathetic to the Nazis or Ustachi. Since no one came out to greet them, they felt it best just to keep walking. At the edge of the town, the airmen came upon an open field within a hundred yards of a small hillside. It was very unsettling being out in the open. Now they were without any forest to hide in should a German or Ustachi patrol suddenly appear. They pondered going back into town and seeking help from any one of the civilian population that might be willing to come out from hiding behind their curtains. Suddenly, a soldier in a German uniform appeared from the other side of the hill and yelled "HALT!!" The airmen froze as ordered. Collectively, each of the Americans and their Italian friend felt their stomachs sink into despair. Sgt. Gourley looked over to Sgt. White and said,"I thought we were going to make it?"

After a short time of staring at the airmen, the soldier called for the men to advance. The airmen nervously advanced with their hands in the air. As the soldier came closer, he lowered his weapon. He was speaking to them in a foreign language that only since they crash landed seemed strangely familiar if not odd coming from a German soldier. The Italian civilian started yelling "Americans Americanas!!" Lt. Escardo told the Italian to keep quiet. But the Italian was the first one to recognize the soldier's accent as not being German, but Slavic! The soldier ran up to the Italian and said "Americano??" Soon the crew realized he was a Yugoslavian that was conscripted into the German army. After a bit of careful translating, the soldier explained that he had deserted the battlefront and was planning on joining the Partisans in their fight against the Nazis. The soldier was forced into the German army during the beginning of the occupation. He didn't seem to be a die-hard communist but rather decided to act as one, so he could join the Partisans without prosecution. And the best news for the American airmen was that he said he could lead them to the Partisans in another nearby village. The soldier then proceeded to lead the crew in a northerly direction back through the town. As they walked, passing through the town again, they continued down a narrow road, leaving the town continuing north. After walking for a couple of hours, they reached the small village of only a few cottages. It was now late in the afternoon. Soon they were greeted by a few civilians who weren't as shy about coming out to see these strangers walking through the village. After a few cautious glances at the Americans, they saw that they weren't Germans and they started smiling and greeted the airmen with cheer and extending their arms out to shake hands with the Americans. The villagers had no idea that the airmen were lost and trying to get out of Yugoslavia. But their warm greeting lifted the crew's spirit. It was as if they were arriving as a small contingent of American liberators to help the Partisans force a retreat of the Nazis. In reality, it was the crew who were just as in need of seeking liberation. Liberation from two months of constant nervous stress caused by hiding from the enemy, being on the run while evading capture, constant hunger, lice, aches and pains, and pure exhaustion brought on by traveling what amounted to hundreds of miles on foot, much of the mileage accumulated during failed escape attempts to Pranjani across rugged mountainous terrain when led by the Chetnik escorts. And in freezing weather much of the time. But now in the company of the villagers, the crew began to feel their luck may have changed for the better.

One of the civilians made note that they were on the side of the Partisans, but not much in favor of communism from an idealistic point of view. For this half of the crew, they would soon learn that while some supporters of the Partisans believed in communism, others were privately reluctant about this ideology. But it was better to support Tito's communist leadership and its resistance forces openly than to live (or die) under the fascist Ustachis and the German occupiers. In other words for some Partisan supporters, only behind closed doors would they admit their dislike towards being labeled a communist. They were simply trying to survive and the communist led Partisans were their best option for survival. They would rather live under Tito's communist rule for the time being as long as the Partisans were successful in the fight against their greater threat, the Fascists and the Serbian Chetniks whom they believed were only interested in creating a greater Serbia and therefore subjecting any non-Serb in support of the Partisans or Ustachi to ethnic cleansing. But they could never admit out loud that they were not in favor of Tito and his communist rule because that alone could subject them to execution. So for these individuals, it came down to aligning themselves with the Partisans or face imprisonment or death. And the Partisans were winning the fight. The Serbian population was also a victim of ethnic cleansing by the Ustachis. The atrocities committed by both sides during the second world war are staggering. Both in the numbers killed and in the brutality of these murders which included innocent men, women, and children.

Others were faithfully supporting Tito, since Tito's leadership was founded on socialist ideology rather than ethnicity. For that he won support that crossed national lines. The result was Tito being able to count on some level of Partisan support in every corner of the country. So if a communist the likes of Josip Tito promised to rid their country of the Nazi occupiers and their puppet regime, the brutal Ustachi's forces, then Tito was the man a large portion of the population had no choice but to accept as their leader. As for the devoted monarchist, ethnic Serbian Chetniks, they became less involved and were seen as unsuccessful in the fight against the Fascists and were strongly in opposition to socialism. To the Partisan forces they in turn thought of them as traitors and unwilling to unite outside of Serbian territories. Even though the Chetniks also strongly opposed common enemies like the anti-Serbian Ustachi and Nazi fascism, with exception to those Chetniks who at times collaborated with the German's fight against the Partisans believing the Nazi's were the lesser evil. The hard lined three-way division between the  Partisans, Chetniks, and Ustachis, really amounted to a civil war between a socialist ideology and its desire to split up Serbian land and divide it among mixed ethnic groups, versus a single ethnic Serbian hold on land they rightfully owned for many generations. This explains why they fiercely opposed one another. Throw in the fascist Ustachi regime and their favoring of the conquering Nazi occupiers and the whole country was turned into a war torn geopolitical mess. For the crew it made it difficult to put their trust in anyone in the country. But they had been briefed on the Partisans back at their base and knew that they might be their best hope at getting back to Italy. And that was their only concern. Getting back to their airbase at Sterparone and then eventually home to the States.

Lieutenants Keane and Escardo and the rest of the group at least felt a bit of optimism that they would soon be in good hands, or at least more reliable hands than in the care of the ineffective Chetnik soldiers. They were surprised that they had reached their objective sooner than expected after splitting up from the other group earlier that morning. Lieutenants Keane and Escardo and the rest of their group could now only hope that their comrades led by Lieutenants Grossman and Daniels in the other group would be so fortunate. The soldier who met the crew on the hillside led the airmen to a house where they were introduced to a Partisan soldier. He then asked the group to follow him to an adjoining room where Escardo and Keane reported to a seemingly uninterested Partisan officer who began questioning the American officers. Even though the crew felt that all would go well from here on out, they still wanted to make sure they were among friendlies who could help them. The bottom line was they needed to establish some trust. Fortunately, the Partisan officer spoke some English. "You are American's, no? What unit are you with" said the officer. After a bit of hesitation to answer, the airmen looked around and soon trust was established after viewing some of the Partisan soldiers wearing American issue Army boots and unmarked green field jackets. "First Lt. Thomas J. Keane, USAAF, 483$^{rd}$ bombardment group, 840$^{th}$ squadron" replied Lt. Keane. "Second Lt. Carlos A. Escardo, USAAF" added the co-pilot. "Were you shot down while dropping us supplies?" asked the Partisan officer. "No, we were on a bombing mission to knock out the oil refinery at Vienna. We were low on fuel and oxygen after the leaving the target area and were hit by flak causing a fuel and oxygen leak forcing us to crash land near Banja Luca" explained Lt. Escardo. "We've been evading capture for the past two months," said Lt. Keane. The rest of the crew gave the Partisan officer their names and ranks. Lt. Escardo informed the Partisan officer that they had split up into two groups earlier that morning and that there were six more of the crew seeking the aide of the Partisans. He asked if they had heard anything of their whereabouts.

"No, not yet. But do not worry. We have forced most of the Germans to retreat north out of Zepec, Teslic and most of the southern region. Only Chetniks and small pockets of Ustachi remain" said the officer. The airmen were careful not to speak of their time with the Chetniks, especially not mentioning Mr. and Mrs. Cvijanovic because they understood the deep rooted division between the Partisans and Chetniks. Though they had had their misgivings towards the Chetnik soldiers, they still felt greatly indebted towards the Cvijanovic family for hiding them at their farm for so long. Any mention of Chetniks and or the Cvijanovic's might subject them to persecution by the communist regime. Much in the same way they learned to avoid talk of seeking help from the Partisans while in the company of the Chetnik escorts. The rest of the questioning resulted in the Americans giving vague answers. Mostly talking about basic things like their hometowns in America or their duties on their B-17 bomber. After the brief questioning the airmen billeted in an old chicken shed where they could rest and spend the night before moving out to another Partisan camp further from the battlefront. Later that evening, they were joined by a group of captured German soldiers. The crew were not thrilled by the prisoner's presence and having to share their sleeping quarters as primitive as they were, with the enemy. The Germans huddled on the far end of the coup and pretty much kept to themselves. They looked as ragged and tired as the airmen looked. It wasn't long before both parties settled and fell asleep.

At dawn a Partisan officer accompanied by a few armed soldiers roused the Germans awake and led them out of the shed at gunpoint. The startled American airmen felt relieved that the Germans were removed from their presence. Then about a half hour later, they heard simultaneous gunshots. After a short time had passed, one of the Partisan soldiers who marched the Germans out of the shed returned without the prisoners. Figuring that the German prisoners had just been executed, the airmen were left wondering what the Partisans had in store for them? "Are we next?" Sgt. Gourley wondered out loud. Their moment of doubt dispelled when the soldier motioned for the crew to join him for a breakfast of bean soup that did little to fill their empty stomachs. It seemed the Partisans were only offering a small portion of food to the very hungry airmen because they reserved most of their food supplies for their soldiers. The crew was told to sit tight while arrangements would be made to get them to an airfield where they would be evacuated.

Meanwhile a day earlier the other half of the crew which was led by Lieutenants

Grossman and Daniels, had been up in the mountain ridge moving south all day. They walked until sunset and darkness overcame the day. They noticed a small village about a half mile ahead in the distance. They could make out a group of cottages. The village seemed deserted. Only the sight of smoke exiting the chimneys gave them any signs of life. Everything was eerily quiet. Feeling leery about entering the village until they were sure it was safe, they looked around and noticed a single farmhouse hidden off the trail about hundred yards off the trail. Lt. Grossman conferred with Lt. Daniels. "What do you think?" He asked Lt. Daniels. "Well maybe we can check out that farmhouse. Maybe someone there can help us or at least give us something to eat. I'm starving!" said Lt. Daniels. "Well they could also be housing some Germans. But then again they might be able to help us find the Partisans" responded Lt. Grossman. The rest of the crew, Sargents LeClair, Baker, Taxel and the B-24 crew member Sgt. Whetstone pleaded with Lt. Grossman to risk approaching the farmhouse. Lt. Grossman told the crew, "OK, those of you who have your sidearms, be ready just in case." With that, the airmen went up to the house and tapped on the front door.

A middle-aged looking farmer cracked the door open a slit and peeked at the men at his front door. "Hello, we are Americans. Do you speak English?" asked Lt. Daniels speaking slowly and deliberately. "Uh, er little English yes. Amerikano? "Yes, Amerikano!" replied Lt. Daniels. "Please come, come" said the farmer motioning with hand gestures for the crew to enter his house. He introduced them to his wife who was washing cooking utensils. Sgt. Whetstone looked at the woman and asked if they had any food they could spare. The woman who spoke no English just stared at the men. "Yes, we have little food to give" said the farmer. He then told his wife to offer the men some of the bread that they had baked earlier. It wasn't much to eat, but to the practically starving crew, each bite was pure heaven! It was most likely a good thing they didn't have much to eat. While the men were dealing with various ailments, they weren't too bad off all things considered.But if they had been given too much food too quickly their stomach problems might only have become worse. As the airmen chewed on the bread, Lt. Grossman spoke to the farmer. "Could you tell us if the village ahead is Partisan?" he asked. At first the farmer seemed reluctant to tell him or any of the crew anything about the village. Finally he said that the town down the road was occupied by a population sympathetic to the Partisans. That was all the crew had to hear. Now they were convinced that they would eventually make it back to Italy.

The mood was practically jubilant. Before the men finished eating, the door swung open and several soldiers entered through the front door as if they were expected by the farmer and his wife. In the dimly lit interior they appeared to be Germans. The airmens' collective cheer turned to fear. But as the soldiers came closer to the light of the fire they were recognized by the crew as Chetniks. The fear turned to anger and frustration. The presence of Chetniks did not please Lt. Grossman or the rest of the crew. Now they were as bad off as they were before, the entire crew thought to themselves. The Chetnik who seemed to be a Sargent in charge of this group spoke English. He told the Americans to come with them to their outpost up in the interior of the mountains. But Lt. Grossman had no intention of going anywhere with the Chetniks but kept his feelings quiet for the time being. He had given the Chetniks their chance to evacuate he and his crew for two unsuccessful months and wasn't about to take any orders from these or any Chetnik soldiers any longer. "We have been walking all day and are very tired. We need to rest. Couldn't we wait until morning?" suggested Lt. Grossman. The farmer offered his house to the airmen to spend the night. The Chetnik Sargent agreed. The Chetnik soldiers were as tired as the Americans. The farmer and his wife went off the bed and the crew and their unwanted Chetnik friends found a place on the floor to sleep.

## *Chapter 13*

Approximately six o'clock the next morning of March 13th, the Chetnik soldiers woke the airmen in preparation to head to their outpost. Lieutenants Grossman and Daniels got the rest of the crew up and had them gather outside with the Chetniks who began leading them down to the road. As the Chetnik soldiers turned to walk in the opposite direction of the village, Lt. Grossman motioned for his crew to follow him. So the airmen split off and turned and started walking away from the Chetnik soldiers and right towards the town. "Where are you going? Our headquarters is THIS way" said the Chetnik Sargent pointing over his shoulder. But the airmen kept on walking towards the town. At first, the Chetnik's thought the Americans were joking. When they realized the airmen were not joking, the Sargent ordered the Americans to stop. A couple of the Chetniks lowered their rifles from their shoulders and attempted to stop them at gunpoint. But Lt. Grossman decided to call the soldier's bluff. "Keep moving" he ordered his crewmen. "Halt!"shouted the Sargent. But without turning their heads, the Americans kept walking away. Then one of the Chetniks attempted to fire his weapon, but as he pulled the trigger the gun jammed. "Halt!" the Sargent shouted again. The desperate Americans just ignored his command and then started running. Suddenly one of the younger Chetnik soldiers, who barely looked eighteen years of age, fired his rifle at the crew nearly striking Sgt. Baker. He felt the heat of the bullet whiz by his hand. Sgt. Baker still had his sidearm and almost took it out and fired back but thought it might only get some of his comrades shot. Lt. Grossman and the rest of the crew stopped running and briefly froze after hearing the shot. Lt. Grossman turned around angrily facing the Chetnik Sargent. "If you don't let us go, I will make sure our American government hears about a Chetnik soldier firing on an American soldier, and that will only bring trouble to your cause. You understand me?" The Chetnik Sargent hesitated, giving thought to Lt. Grossman's threat before ordering his men to stand down. Deep down he knew Lt. Grossman was right. As much as he hated the Americans going over to the Partisans for help in evacuation, he knew that any news of a Chetnik soldier purposely harming or killing any American would greatly lessen their country's chances of building a strong relationship with the Western Allies should they need their support against the Communist once the Germans were defeated. It was a bold move on the part of Lt. Grossman to verbally threaten a Chetnik soldier. But with the Partisan line within reach, he remembered what Mr. Cvijanovic had told him about the Chetniks lacking the resources get them out of Yugoslavia or even through to Mihailovic's headquarters in Pranjani. The crew had already lost faith in any use of the Chetniks as a means of getting back to their base in Italy. No one was in the mood for false promises of rescue from any Chetnik soldiers, regardless of how well their intent might be, or not. Had they crash landed near Pranjani, their odds of being evacuated with the help of the Serbian Chetniks would have been much greater. But the airfield at Pranjani was located in what is now Serbia, and the crew was in what is today known as Bosnia-Herzegovina, far from Mihailovic's Chetnik post.

"You are crazy if you think you will find help in the village. Go ahead Lieutenant, we will not stop you. But you are now on your own. If the Germans or the Ustachi capture you, no one can help you." said the Sargent in a resigned but serious tone. After this frightening ordeal the airmen wondered if the farmer had set them up. They began to question his intent. Why did the Chetnik soldiers just happen to show up at his front door last night? Were the Americans being followed on the mountain trails? The crew also questioned why would a Chetnik fire on the very people they were supposedly trying to save? And yet they relented and let the men go at the mere mention of informing the US government of their use of firearms against the airmen. Perhaps the Chetnik Sargent came to his senses and realized it was not worth the risk of facing his superiors having to explain their actions taken towards the Americans. One thing Lt. Grossman and the crew believed was the great odds that Partisans sympathizers were indeed in the village. The key to this belief was how adamant the Chetnik Sargent was on insisting they go in the opposite direction of the town. Though Chetniks and Partisans were often nearby at times, they were still in a battle for gaining rule in the country. And with the Partisans and Russians making successful advances against the Germans, the Chetniks were careful about entering towns and villages known to have a majority of supporters of Tito's communist influence or those providing aid to Partisan soldiers.

As Lt. Grossman's group approached the outskirts of the village, it appeared almost deserted. The street was quiet this early morning. Only the lazy puffs of chimney smoke from a few of the cottages indicated any sign of life. Occasionally a door would open a crack, or a curtain would be pulled back slightly from a window. Just like the other group the day before in Zepec, they were feeling quite anxious knowing they were being watched without being able to see who was peering through the windows and door cracks. After four years of occupation and war, most of the smaller towns and village's civilian population in Yugoslavia were hesitant about greeting any strangers in uniform until they were sure they were not a threat. They continued walking almost at a casual pace passing a few cottages. Eventually, an old man ventured out of his home and approached the Americans. After some effort attempting to understand the man's Slavic language, he finally informed the airmen he was sided with the Partisans. Lt. Grossman and crew looked at each other and smiled, grinning ear to ear! They had finally achieved their goal of reaching a Partisan controlled village. The old man pointed to a house near the end of the road and conveyed that there were more Partisans that could help them. After walking further into the village they approached the house when suddenly a few Partisans soldiers came out. "We are Americana," said Lt. Grossman to one of the soldiers. "You are American??" responded the young soldier in English. "Yes, American!!" responded Lt. Daniels. "Our plane crashed near Banja Luca, and we are trying to find help getting back to our base in Italy" he added. "Can you tell us where we can find help getting out of the country?" asked Lt. Grossman. "We came from a Partisan camp about 3 miles from here a few days ago. We are due back today" said the young man. " We will take you there" he added. It was the best news Lt. Grossman and his group had heard in quite some time. All the men felt a great sense of joy as they were escorted towards the camp, although the excitement was somewhat muted when they thought about the whereabouts of the other group they split up from the day before. They had no idea what might have happened to the group led by Lieutenants Keane and Escardo. Were they successful reaching the Partisans? Or were they captured or killed by retreating Germans or Ustachis? These thoughts weighed heavily on Lt. Grossman's mind. Splitting up evading crews is never encouraged according to the USAAF training guidelines. Unless crews bail out and are scattered over enemy territory, crews are thought to be much more resourceful if they all stick together. Lt. Grossman could only hope he would eventually reunite with the other group sooner or later. Three of his comrades soon joined the Partisan soldier and they escorted the airmen through the rest of the village and down the road exiting the town.

Later that morning at around eleven o'clock, the group reached Zepec. "We must report in here and gather some food and water before continuing towards our camp. We must also make sure the road is safe for travel before heading out to the camp" said the Partisan soldier. The Partisans led the airmen to the same house where Lieutenants Keane, Escardo and the rest of their group were waiting. As they walked through the door, Lt. Grossman and his group glanced in the direction of the other room and saw Lt. Keane and immediately shouted, "Tom!" Lt. Keane looked up and saw his pilot and navigator along with the rest of his comrades entering the room. "Bob! Sandy!! You guys made it!" he called out to his fellow officers. Within seconds the reunited crewmen were laughing and joking and back slapping each other. Sgt. Sparks was overjoyed. "What took you so long!" he joked. "We thought you guys might have been captured!" "We thought the same thing about you guys!" replied Sgt. LeClair. Sgt. Whetstone called out to his fellow B-24 crew member Cpl. Howe, "Hey Bobby, over here!" The crew was very relieved to be all together again even if they had only been split up for a day and a half. But knowing the enemy was fighting nearby, being separated for thirty-five minutes let alone thirty-five hours could have had led to tragic results for either group and each man knew it. Meanwhile the Partisan soldier was speaking to some of his comrades to gather some intelligence regarding whether or not the road to the camp was clear of any Germans or Ustachi at present. After glancing over a map of the area showing last known positions of the enemy, it was decided to be relatively safe to proceed to the camp but to use caution. The celebration between the reunited crew soon settled down as the Partisan soldier asked the Americans to fall in and prepare to march off to the Partisan's camp which was near the town of Tesanj, approximately fifteen miles away to the north which would translate to an eight or nine-hour march on a good day. There the airmen could meet with his superiors who could perhaps assist in evacuating the crew out of the country. Ironically, Tesanj and the town of Teslic were located in separate valleys divided by the small branch of the mountain range the crew was trekking through before splitting up. The two towns were about seven miles apart. Had they known and continued on the east from the vicinity of Teslic, they would have only a few short miles before reaching the other side of the mountain range and to the Partisan camp in the valley below near Tesanj. Indeed the crew had reached their objective, and both groups were back together at that. But the idea of marching on sore and tired feet caused more than a bit of grumbling among the men especially upon learning from their Partisan escorts that they were being moved out in a northwesterly direction. The same general direction from which they had already walked.

Lt. Grossman and crew were hoping that they would continue south towards the Dalmatian coast along the Adriatic Sea. Much of that coastal region had been seized by the Yugoslavian Partisans from the Fascist Italians and the Nazi backed Ustachi forces after Mussolini's removal from power including the major port cities of Zadar and Split. In fact the Allies bombed Zadar to nearly complete ruin causing a mass exodus of the remaining Italian population. With its destruction Zadar became known as the "Dresden" of the Adriatic. Lt. Grossman conferred with the Partisan soldiers and asked why couldn't they continue south towards the coast? The Partisan just casually pointed over his shoulder to the north and replied,"because our camp is this way." That answer didn't sit well with the crew who by now was beyond exhausted from all the walking they had done going back to late January after their crash landing. They were not looking forward to another long march back up the mountain. To the crew, it felt somewhat like going in circles. "Do not worry Lieutenant, this is the best way if you want to avoid the battlefront. There is much fighting against the enemy, and it would be too dangerous. You must stay in the mountains to safely reach Tesanj." The crew was in no position to argue. Just as when they first crashed and were picked up by Chetnik soldiers, they would again have to trust a local renegade army. At least now they were putting their trust for repatriation in the hands of a faction that were gaining more control of the region as more and more Germans and Ustachis' were retreating not only from the Partisans but also from the Russians closing in from the east. The Partisans appeared to be a better organized unit compared to the Chetniks. While the Chetniks operated as a uniformed resistance with ranks and tactical combat operations, they lacked many of the necessities and regulations that regular armies have. They didn't participate in certain military regulations such as soldiers keeping their hair short, marching and/or drilling on a regular basis. The Chetniks lived among the civilian population with no official military base of operation. They mostly operated out of small abandoned houses used as outposts such as the ones the crew was well familiar with back near Celiniac. The lack of allied support caused their overall deficiencies. The Chetniks were also weakened by the split within the Serbian population, some staying loyal to Mihailovic while others turned to another Chetnik leader Milan Nedic. Nedic was in collaboration with the Nazi's due in part because he felt the Germans were the lesser evil to that of the socialist Partisans. The Partisans operated much in the same way the Chetniks did by way of guerrilla style warfare but on a much larger scale. Many of the Partisan soldiers lived in encampments near towns or villages. Other Partisans on occasion used local shops or barns as headquarters. They looked as gruff as the Chetniks, but were more consistently uninformed with the majority of them groomed with short hair and clean shaven. The service hats they wore were similar to the ones the Chetnik soldiers wore with the exception that the Partisans hat featured a bright red Communist star emblem on the front. They also had women in uniform fighting alongside the men in combat which would come as quite a surprise to the American airmen. Women serving in combat was unheard of to Americans of 1945. But it was quite common in the Russian and Yugoslavian armies. Now the only question remaining was would the help of these Partisans lead the crew to an eventual return to their base?

*Chapter 14*

Just after noon a contingent of four Partisan soldiers began marching the crew out of the town and up the road about a mile. They came upon a small bridge that crossed the Bosna river. The Americans marched in two's as in a common military fashion. Two Partisans in front with two covering the rear. Three of the soldiers were armed with rifles, one of them armed with an automatic machine gun that may have been Russian made. They crossed the bridge and were heading towards a trail that would lead them up the mountain when a couple of American P-47 fighter planes were spotted by the crew flying fast and low directly towards them. Sgt. Gourley, walking alongside Sgt. White said to him,"I don't think they realize we're Americans!" The words no sooner left his lips when the plane's guns opened fire! "Take cover!!" shouted Lt. Grossman. The crew, along with the Partisan soldiers, immediately scrambled and dove off to the side of the road and hid in the brush as bullets from each of the American fighters eight .50 caliber machine guns riddled the road about one hundred and fifty feet past their present location. Fortunately for the crew and their escorts, the pilot's trajectory was off, sparing them from being killed or wounded by friendly fire. As the plane's engines roared above as they flew over the hiding men, they opened fire again on the bridge and destroyed it. The fighters were most likely returning from a strafing mission on the railroad bridges in Zagreb, about one hundred miles northwest and were looking for targets of opportunity while on their way back to their base in Italy. Thinking the marching crew was a small group of retreating Germans, they decided to try and take them out. "Is everybody ok?" asked Lt. Grossman. "Yeah, I think so" replied Lt. Keane. "What in the hell! Couldn't they see we were wearing American flight suits!" Lt. Daniels said out of desperation. "Lucky for us their aim was off" replied Sgt. LeClair. "Well they sure shot up that bridge to hell" added Sgt. Taxel. Then the leader of the Partisan escorts spoke up. "We were told your Air force has been attacking German positions to the north to cut off supply or retreat routes from the south. But this is the first time I witness an attack along the river Bosna" he said.

Everyone was a bit shaken up by their first encounter with friendly fire. An air crew's war was always in the air destroying enemy targets thirty thousand feet below and dodging flak bursts and German fighter attacks. But at least they had a bomber formation's wall of fifty caliber machine guns to defend themselves. Now the crew had the misfortune of experiencing, however brief, what it was like to become a ground target for a couple of American fighter pilots who mistook their identity. With no time to delay, the Partisan escorts expressed the need to get a move on quickly. The Americans dusted themselves off and continued walking.

They came upon the trail to the mountain range and started up its fairly steep ascent. Fortunately, the range at this point only peaked at just under seventeen hundred feet, so though it was hard on their sore feet, the high point of the trail was reached in less than an hour. The advantage of walking along the mountain range was the ground cover of taller trees. The same tree cover they experienced on most of their mountain treks while missing in action. The crew always felt safer up above the valleys than on the main roads that were still being used by pockets of Germans and Ustachi patrols. Even though the Germans were retreating north, they were still fighting as they retreated. The crew marched on. They were still walking in two's as if they were practicing their marching in formation drills back in the States during basic training.

Sargents Taxel and Lt. Escardo, in particular, were feeling increasingly ill with stomach ailments caused by the lack of decent food and exhaustion. And Sgt. Baker's feet were starting to bleed, and he was fearing he might be developing trench foot. However every time the men rested he took off his boots and exposed his feet to keep them dry using whatever heat that was generated from the sunlight to warm them. In fact all of the men followed suit and would remove their boots allowing their feet to feel the fresh mountain air. The key to avoiding trench foot was to keep your feet dry. Had they not exposed their feet to the sun, the threat of trench foot was a real possibility, especially while walking through snow and mud caused by the warming temperatures as springtime approached.

The crew had been walking for approximately seven hours when they reached the point of decent off the mountain. The trail began lowering the group down to the valley below. They seemed rejuvenated as they reached the bottom and one of the Partisan soldiers exclaimed, "Tesanj! Our camp is just beyond those trees" he said as he pointed towards a group of fir trees in the near distance.

As night fell on March 13th, they entered a camp that was occupied by about forty Partisan soldiers. They were shown to a tent that resembled a U.S. Army issue field tent. Sgt. Gourley noticed something peculiar in a nearby harvest wagon. The wooden wagon was filled with U.S. Army clothing and combat boots! Walking the entire time in uncomfortable flight boots after his regular boots were stolen back at the Chetnik outpost almost three months earlier, he asked the Partisan soldier if he could grab a pare for himself.

"Ne" (no), these are for the soldiers," the Partisan told him. Sgt. Gourley couldn't believe it. He thought to himself. "There must be two hundred pairs of boots on that wagon, and they can't part with a few pairs?" Sgt. Baker spoke up,"Here, I'll trade you my boots," he said sarcastically as he lifted one leg off the ground exposing his worn out, filthy flight boots. The Partisan soldier only looked away ignoring Sgt. Baker as if seeing soldiers worn out footwear was nothing out of the ordinary.

A Partisan officer came over to the crew. "You shall stay here for a while and rest and join us for a meal. In two hours we will take you to Teslic" he told them. "You will spend the night there." The twelve Americans along with their Italian friend gathered in line with other Partisan soldiers and were handed some bread to chow on. Lt. Grossman asked the Partisan officer about Teslic. "Is Teslic safe for us?" he asked. Lt. Grossman thought to himself about the Chetnik who said he would go for help in Teslic. Everyone in the crew was under the impression that at least part of Teslic had a fair influence of Chetniks. The very group they took great lengths to break away from a few days earlier. The last thing Lt. Grossman and the crew wanted was to get caught in the middle of a gunfight between the Partisans and the Chetniks. "Yes, you will be safe in Teslic" the Partisan officer reassured the Americans. "There are other Partisans there who will help you to continue on your journey. We are just a small outfit that must stay and hold and rid Tesjani of traitors." The Partisan officer then excused himself and ordered one of the escorts to prepare a detail to escort the crew to Teslic. "What's he mean by traitors?" Sgt. White asked Lt. Grossman. "I don't know Sargent, probably Chetniks. Listen up men, don't forget, not one word about our receiving any aid from any Chetnik. Are we clear?" whispered Lt. Grossman, keeping his voice low to avoid alerting the Partisans milling around. Everyone in the crew nodded an affirmative. Sgt. Baker spoke up. "Lieutenant, it seems like we are just going around in circles. Just like it was with the Chetniks. I mean didn't we just skirt around Teslic a couple of days ago, and know we are going back in that direction tonight? Shouldn't we be heading towards the coast? Sir, how do we know these Partisans are even going to be able to get us out of the country?" "He's right Lieutenant" added Sgt. Taxel.

"Are we any better off now than we were back at the Mr. Cvijanovic's farm?" "Listen up Sargent," said Lt. Grossman. "We gave the Chetniks two months after they promised to get us out in a week after we crashed, and where did that get us? And we couldn't stay with the Cvijanovic's any longer. It was too dangerous for them, and us. Now we've only been with these Partisans for a few days. Let's just go along with them, wherever they take us to. We have no choice. The Chetniks had their chance. We'll just have to put our trust in the Partisans for now." he said.

At around eleven o'clock that evening, the Partisan officer informed the crew that it was time to move out to Teslic. The distance was only about five miles west of Tesjani, but many of the crew were still suffering severe exhaustion despite getting a bit more nourishment from the Partisans at their camp. Everyone in the group had lost a noticeable amount of weight. Only their will buoyed by thoughts of getting back home to their loved ones continued to give them the strength to march on. The married crewmen such as Lt. Grossman, Sargents White, Baker and Taxel would often speak about their longing to get back to their wives while the rest of the crew would try not to think about how worried their mothers must be with their boys listed as missing. Lt. Escardo in particular was very concerned about his family in Peru. He parents were under the impression that their son was not flying combat missions. Only his brother was informed of his missing in action. On more than one occasion, he expressed his worry about his parents. "My Mother and Father must be crying every day" Lt. Escardo confided to Lt. Keane. "I never told them I requested flying combat missions. They thought I would be only flying supplies within the U.S." "Why didn't you tell them?" asked Lt. Keane. "I can't imagine what my Mother and Father would feel, you know, getting an MIA telegram all the while thinking I was flying stateside" he added. Lt. Escardo replied "I wanted to do my part after your country gave me the opportunity to fly passenger planes, but if I had told my parents I would be flying in combat it would have upset them more than you could know." They may have contacted the Pentagon and using their connections in Washington, had me grounded or sent back to Peru! I only told my brother about my combat flying so if anything happened to me he would let my parents know at the appropriate time I'm sure." he added.

The men formed up as usual with the four Partisan soldiers continuing as the guides. They walked through the valley in the darkness of night to avoid any Ustachi patrols, something they had all grew accustomed to throughout the several miles of walking since they crash landed. But most of the enemy patrols had retreated north with the Germans. In reality the crew most likely could have waited until daylight to march on to Teslic and would have arrived without any incident. But the Partisans weren't taking any chances. They wanted to take the crew to Teslic as soon as possible and turn the Americans over to higher ranking Partisan officers who were better qualified in regards to rescuing downed allied airmen. Their superiors in Teslic could decide when and where the crew would need to go from there to eventual evacuation out of Yugoslavia. After about three hours of walking the crew reached Teslic and another Partisan encampment. During the night at most of their camps, the Partisan soldiers would take turns sleeping in small groups on the ground or in small pup tents, while others stood to watch. The Partisan escorts met with another Partisan who acted as a sentry at the edge of the encampment. After speaking to the guard, he had another soldier on watch summon a Partisan officer. Soon after, a Partisan officer came over and greeted the crew. Lt. Grossman, in turn, introduced himself as the pilot officer of the crew. The Partisan officer seemed friendly enough. He offered the crew water and a small bit of bean and fat soup which again lacked the slightest amount of salt, as usual. The Officer took the crew to a somewhat larger tent and presented the crew to the ranking officer. It is believed he was a Major, but his name isn't known or remembered. The Major interrogated the crew. After the brief interrogation he spoke to them in English. "I can help you get back to Italy, but you must first get to the village of Travnik. There is a British mission that was put in place there recently since the Germans and Ustachis retreated north. We have information that the British have an airfield near the village. We will leave after we can make arrangements to escort you there." "How long will it take to make these arrangements?" asked Lt. Escardo "It may some time. We have some escorts who are due to arrive back here in three or four days. They will take you to the airfield. For now, you must stay and rest. We can spare little food, but there will be enough for all of you." "How far is Travnik?"asked Lt. Grossman. "It is about fifty kilometers south of here. It will take a few days." said the officer. Travnik had been a Nazi and Ustachi occupied village and starting in late August 1941 was the scene of the mass arrest and eventual exterminations of mostly Jewish women and children at the nearby concentration camp Kruscica, located about 10 miles from Travnik. But as with many villages in Yugoslavia in 1945, the successful Partisan advance from the south caused many Ustachis to abandoned the village and retreat with their German allies to the north as they became outnumbered by the growing and well supported Partisan forces. As parts of Yugoslavia were being liberated from Nazi control, British and American forces began dropping in military personnel to help the Partisans secure safe zones for downed Allied air crews. The allies called the outposts "missions." The plan was to set up temporary airstrips similar to the airfield at Pranjani that was guarded by Mihailovic's Chetniks.

Finally on Tuesday morning of March 20th, the crew was told to assemble for the long walk to Travnik. Another group of four Partisan soldiers joined them as escorts. The weather was fair, and the crew was practically walking on automatic. Not much was said as they prepared for the long journey. The optimism the men had felt before when they first came in contact with the Partisans was waning a bit as it seemed they were only going from one Partisan camp to another over the last couple of days. But the sight of Partisans soldiers wearing those American made combat boots and marching all day long at least gave the men hope that they were not far from allied supply drop zones. And by walking in daylight as well as evening hours meant that the risk of capture by the Germans was becoming more unlikely.

Suddenly the crew noticed a group of men coming up to the trail from the side and out of the brush. It was another group of downed American airmen escorted by a single Partisan soldier. The crew couldn't believe their eyes at first. They thought it might be a group of retreating German soldiers or worse yet a Ustachi patrol. But as each of the crew noticed the blue patch with the wings and star of the Army Air Corp on their shoulders, they all drew a sigh of relief. They appeared in much better shape and weren't seemingly suffering from malnutrition and exhaustion as bad as the Grossman crew were. There were eleven American total in this group. Both crews cheerfully greeted each other. "Hi, I'm first pilot Lt.Robert Grossman of the 483[rd.]" "Hi, first pilot Lt. Charles Estes of the 98th" responded the young aviator. "This my crew, Lieutenant's John Congelton, Bob Swain, Ernie Swanson, Joe Dobkin, James Mulligan, Ed Valient and Sargent's John Norris, Raphael Gonyea, Don Brown and Walt Scott. Lt. Grossman and crew began introducing themselves to Lt. Estes and his crew with friendly handshakes, forgetting to mention that they had been dealing with lice. "You boys look a little worn out, if you don't mind my saying," said Lt. Estes. "You guys bailed out?" "No." replied Lt. Grossman. "We crash landed our B-17 near Banja Luca back in January after a raid over Vienna. Our bomb bay doors were frozen shut and we couldn't drop our bomb load. Then we got hit by flak which caused fuel and oxygen leaks and the loss of our #two engine. After dropping down to five thousand feet, we were able to open the bomb bay and after we safetied the fuses, we dropped them in a river. I decided to crash land the ship on a field in three feet of snow. We were picked up by Chetniks right away and were with them for quite some time, but they couldn't get us out of the country. So we took off on our own and made contact with the Partisans about a week and a half ago. We have been walking ever since" he added. "Damn Lieutenant! How in the hell did you fellas evade the enemy for so long?" asked Lt. Congelton. "It wasn't easy but we somehow managed" said Lt. Grossman. "What about you Lt. Estes, what happened?"

"Well, a group of our B-24's got hit pretty hard on a mission on March 15th to hit the marshaling yards near Vienna. We dropped our bombs and were returning when flak open up pretty heavy on our formation somewhere near the Yugoslavian border. A few of us got hit, some pretty bad. Anyway, we lost our numbers two and four engines. I tried to take us as far as I could or where we could reach friendlies before giving the bailout order to the crew. We all got out pretty quick and luckily weren't scattered too far from one another when we hit the ground. We were fortunate to land close to a nearby village where some locals took us to some of Tito's boys. We walked over the mountains northeast of here with the help from these Partisans. This here Partisan is taking us on our leg to Travnik before turning us over to us to more friendlies. They told us there is a British mission at Travnik" said Lt. Estes.

"Travnik? Well, that is where our guides are taking us!" said Lt. Escardo. "Great, we'll tag along with you men!" said Lt. Estes. The lone Partisan soldier who was Lt. Estes and crew's guide had been conversing with the other Partisans and decided to go along figuring he might as well finish the trek as ordered. Most likely he hoped for a better meal in Travnik since he figured the British stocked better food rations than the village he had come from. With the initial chatting concluded, the group which now added up to twenty-four Americans and one Italian, headed down the mountain trail. With strength in numbers Lt. Grossman and crew felt a bit more secure and confident that they would make it to Travnik unharmed.

## *Chapter 15*

The Partisans continued to stay off the main roads and stayed on the lesser used trails. During the afternoon, they all heard the rumble of American bombers flying overhead returning from a bombing mission of Pragersko. The 15th Air Force had sent six hundred and sixty-four B-17 and B-24 bombers on simultaneous missions to bomb targets in Austria, Germany, and Yugoslavia. Lt. Grossman and the rest of the crew had little reaction other than to wonder what targets were hit that day. They could only look skyward with nary a wave knowing the futility of them being spotted, unlike the excitement they all felt when they first spotted their fellow airmen in the skies over Mr. Cvjanovic's farm and tried in vain to signal them. Lt. Estes' crew seemed more interested as a few of his crewmen speculated the B-24's might be from their very own 98th bomb group. As the day came to an end the Partisan soldiers found an abandoned shed where they all could rest and spend the night before continuing on the following day. Lt. Estes conversed with Lt. Grossman. "Some of your crewmen look like they've seen better days." "Yeah, well, we've been through a lot this past couple of months, but we're hanging in there" replied Lt. Grossman. "Well you let me know if we can be of any help to your men along the trail" offered Lt. Estes. "Thanks, Lieutenant" answered Lt. Grossman. By the way, who's the civilian in your group?" asked Lt. Estes. " Oh, he's an Italian who joined us at the farm. He wants to return to the old country and since we're going his way, well he just tagged along" "Do you think he's a deserter?" asked Lt. Estes." "Does it matter?" replied Lt. Grossman. "I suppose not," said Lt. Estes with a chuckle. "Well I think I need to speak with my crew to check on everyone's morale. I imagine we still have a ways to go" Lt. Grossman added. Sgt. Baker was trying hard to continue walking with his feet aching and Lt. Grossman wanted to make sure he could go on the next day. "How are you feeling Baker?" he asked. "My feet are in pretty bad shape, Lieutenant" replied the Sargent. "Well hang on. If there is an airstrip near Travnik, we'll be back at our base in no time" Lt. Grossman said assuredly. Sgt. Taxel and Lt. Escardo were looking more pale than usual from the exhaustion and malnutrition. Both complained of stomach pains but both vowed they could continue walking. Lt. Keane and Sgt. LeClair were fairly fit but were looking slimmer than before. Lt. Daniels was anxious. He felt bad that he was mistaken about their plane's location, believing they were over Italy near friendly outposts when they crash landed. Lt.

Daniels never was blamed publicly nor deserved such by any of his fellow crew members. There were many factors that led the crew to becoming MIA's. For instance he had no control over the frozen bomb bay doors or the leaking fuel and oxygen lines, or the overcast skies that limited much of the ground visibility until they dropped down to five thousand feet. Still he felt a strong sense of responsibility for his miscalculation as to their location when they crashed. He wanted to make it up to the crew and do his part to help make sure they all got home safely, despite the predicament they all had found themselves in for the past couple of months. So he especially was counting on the Partisans to aid them in their safe return to Italy. The truth is that no matter who the navigator was on their last mission, their situation wouldn't have been much different under the circumstances. They lost too much fuel to have any chance of making back to their base. They had landed among friendlies and that was really the best they or any other bomber crew would or could have hoped for under the circumstances.

Sgt. Sparks, White, Gourley, and the B-24 crewmen Sgt. Whetstone and Cpl. Howe were all hanging in there with little complaint knowing that complaining wouldn't do any good, which was remarkable considering their physical deprivation. The young Italian though seemed to be as cheerful as if he had no care in the world. Though he kept to himself most of the time, he seemed to believe as long as he stayed with the Americans things would work out fine. Considering what the Germans were doing to deserting Italians his current predicament was a walk in the park. The next morning on March 21st, the crew again assembled with their Partisan escorts and started off, continuing south towards Travnik and the airfield. The plan was that the Partisans would take the Americans to the makeshift airfield that they believed was still at least a day away from their present location. However, the Partisan officer who ordered the escort to guide the crew to the airstrip was mistaken because the allies had abandoned the airfield's construction due to a lack of communication between themselves and the Partisans about how best to utilize an airstrip that was still technically in a war zone. By late in the afternoon they had walked all day looking but found no such airfield. Now Lt. Grossman and the crew were feeling a bit uneasy towards their Partisan escorts. Was the claim of an airfield that could evacuate them back to Italy turning out to be a false promise? This scenario seemed all too familiar to the crew as they had to deal with promises of evacuation made by the Chetnik soldiers only to have their hopes dashed time and time again.

The Partisan escorts seemed confused. They thought the airfield should have been found by now, but soon they changed their tune regarding the airfield's whereabouts as if to admit they were wrong all along about its location. They hadn't been informed that the airfield had not been built. There was nothing left to do except to rest another night and continue towards Travnik the following morning.

The next day March 22<sup>nd</sup>, the crew spent walking south through the mountain terrain careful to avoid being spotted by retreating Germans and any Ustachis who might be still in the area. They were all getting anxious to reach Travnik as soon as possible. The Partisan soldiers were motioning both crews to pick up the pace. Despite their urgency in reaching the town, many of the crew were still dealing with various foot and stomach ailments and getting little food during the journey certainly did not help. The Partisan soldiers did not have much food or may have been unwilling to share much of what they carried with them. But members from Lt. Estes crew were urging Lt. Escardo and Sargents Baker and Taxel to keep moving forward. Having the fellow American fliers they'd just met encourage the crew was a shot in the arm for them. It resulted in the men being able to keep up with the rest of the crews and therefore covered more distance per each hour. Occasionally the Partisan escorts would approach a farmhouse and ask one of the occupants to offer the passing crew some food and a drink of water. But without the aid of these civilians, there was a good chance they might have become too weak to continue.

Just after sunset on March 22<sup>nd</sup>, both crews finally reach the town of Travnik. The Partisan escorts led them through the town. A villager approached the party after noticing the Partisan soldiers escorting American airmen. One of the Partisans asked the villager to lead them to the British mission they had been briefed about back in Teslic. After walking a couple of blocks the men turned a corner and came to a small building at the end of a dirt street. The villager pointed to the primitive structure. There they were greeted by a British sentry. The crews were now in the hands of a true ally at last. Though Lt. Grossman's crew had little energy to celebrate they all had huge smiles ear to ear on their faces. With little fanfare Lt. Grossman and others from the crew thanked their Partisan escorts for all their help while Lt. Estes and crew did the same. The escorts just smiled and nodded back to the Americans and walked off to join up with another contingent of Partisans who were gathered across the road. Before the crew knew it, they were escorted over to a young British Lieutenant who quickly arranged for some K-rations for the nearly starving airmen. After each crew was finished informally briefing the British Lieutenant on each of their ordeals, a corporal entered with some K-rations for the airmen. There wasn't much food to share since there were many Partisans soldiers to feed, but each of the men in Lt. Grossman and Estes's crew was given the few rations the British could spare, and they immediately began chowing them down with great zeal. Typically the American servicemen found K-rations rather bland and unappealing. But after not eating much of anything the past couple of months, Lt. Grossman and his crew were more than happy to eat the canned food. Suddenly the bland food wasn't so bland after all. "These are the best tasting K-rations I've ever eaten!" said Sgt. Gourley to Sgt White. But because their stomachs had little food for the past couple of months, they became full after only a few bites. Sgt. Taxel and Lt. Escardo along with Sgt. Baker especially barely got past a few swallows before they stopped. They had been having stomach problems more severe than the others and became nauseous as their shrunken stomachs attempted to digest a sudden large swallow of spam. Everyone in Lt. Grossman's crew had to stop eating sooner than they expected. A British medic was summoned to check the men over, and he instructed the men to eat only a very small portion at a time, no matter how hungry they felt. They needed their systems to adjust before eating full square meals. Though none of the men were in a dangerous starvation mode, their lack of any consistent nutrition was still a serious issue they fought through. When they did eat, the portions were rather small. Just enough to sustain them. But they all lost significant weight. Most of the Lt. Grossman's crew were at or below one hundred and twenty pounds at the time they made contact with the Partisans. But as long as they slowly adjusted to the K- rations in smaller portions, they'd tolerate the food and eventually gain back the weight they had lost.

The mission post had been recently set up by the British after Travnik fell to the Partisans, but supplies were at a minimum and mostly reserved for the Partisan fighting units in the area. But while the main purpose of the mission was to support the Yugoslavian Partisans, it was also set up to aid downed allied air crews in the eventual return to their bases in Italy. As word about the location of these allied missions spread among the Partisans, they began to escort more and more downed fliers to these outposts. Most of the missions were established much further east deeper into present-day Serbia after Belgrade was liberated by the combined efforts of the Soviet Red Army, Tito's Partisans, and the Bulgarian Peoples Army in the fall of 1944. A few had airfields attached to serve as bases for the Yugoslavian Partisan's air force. The British even loaned them several Spitfire fighter planes. British and American liaison officers were air dropped off there; some to instruct the Yugoslavian pilots and other officers to coordinate with air drops of supplies and evacuating wounded Partisan soldiers and airlifting allied airmen back to Italy. The mission at Travnik was primitive in relative terms and understaffed in regards to British officers stationed there but at least the roads from Travnik to Split were fairly secure with the heavy presence of the Partisan Army along one of the routes.

## Chapter 16

After the crew had rested a while the British lieutenant informed the two air crews that they had arranged some trucks to transport the men to the town of Split in the morning. Once annexed by fascist Italy along with large parts of Dalmatia, Split had been bombed by the Allies during the Germans re-taking of the town from the Partisans following the Italian capitulation in September of 1943. Split had also been bombed by the Axis forces after the uprising of the very large Croation population who joined up with Tito's Partisans. But by 1945 Split was considered a safe zone and the American air crews knew this. The crew was overjoyed not having to walk the approximately one hundred and eighty miles by way of Mostar to the coastal town. Mostar was a town located southwest of Travnik and had been seized from the Germans and Ustachis and controlled by the Partisans since February of 1945. Though traveling through Mostar was a longer route to Split, it was a much safer route. After a few more bites of K-rations, the crew, along with the B-24 crew of Lt. Estes, hunkered down for the night. Sgt. Gourley took out his pocket bible and read a few passages. He then shared it with a few more crewmen who asked to borrow it for a read. Early the next morning, on March 23rd, two covered American made Dodge trucks pulled up outside the post where the men all spent the night. With a British soldier at the wheel of each truck and with an armed Partisan soldier in the passenger seat and another in the rear bed of the trucks along with the crews, they drove on to Split. With any luck they would be in Spilt before noon. The dirt roads were fairly rough and had to be driven cautiously until they got down out of the mountains. When they reached the coast the trucks turned and headed north along the coast. Sargents LeClair and Sparks marveled at the coastline, the same coastline they had flown over several times as if it was the first time they had ever seen the Adriatic Sea. The smell of sea salt in the air on the coastal portion of their trip reminded the men of the Isle of Capri where they spent time for R&R. Lt. Keane was marking down any towns they passed in a small notebook he had started with the intention of tracking the crew's journey throughout their ordeal in Yugoslavia.

Just after noontime the trucks pulled into Split, once a thriving port in the Kingdom of Yugoslavia before World War Two. In 1925 the Lika railway was completed and henceforth connected Split to the rest of the country making the town an important transportation hub.

Most of the city still showed signs of significant damage due to the four years of on and off bombardment from both sides during the second world war. The British royal navy had occupied part of the harbor in early 1945 to launch rescues at sea of downed airmen who were forced to bail out over the Adriatic and cruisers were used for mine sweeping the coastline. Many Yugoslavians in Split joined up with Tito's communist Partisans to take over the town from the axis powers and the puppet Ustachi fascist regime. Though many local Croatians from Split did not identify themselves as communists, they were strongly anti-Fascist putting them at odds with fellow Croatians who joined or supported the Ustachis. When Tito called on the Croatians not loyal to fascism, to join his Partisans in the fight against the Germans, Italians and Ustachi forces, more than a third of the population of Split joined up to fight.

The Partisans were finally successful on October 26th, 1944 when they captured the town and instituted it as the provisional capital of Croatia to appease the residents who chose to join the fight against Fascism. The Ustachi, who had wanted Split as part of an ethnically pure Nationalist Croatia were forced to retreat north with the Germans. However most were stopped at the Austrian border and captured by the Partisans. Some Ustachis went into hiding and after the war eventually escaped to countries such as Australia, Canada or Germany but most headed for Argentina.

The trucks made their way through Split and proceeded towards the harbor and came to a stop near the wooden piers where they could see a couple of ships anchored along with a few fishing boats docked nearby. The men from both crews disembarked the trucks. Another British officer greeted the Americans and informed them that they would travel to the island of Vis by a boat operated by Tito's makeshift navy made up of Yugoslavian fishermen used to help transport supplies and personal between Vis and Split. The crew would be taken to the island as soon as a boat was available which would be in a day or two. In the meantime the officer directed the men to a building nearby where they could get some rest and relaxation before continuing. Lt. Grossman and his crew were well aware of Vis's strategic importance as a diversionary airstrip for damaged bombers. The crew knew traveling to Vis meant they could fly back to Italy. This information had the crews in near jubilation with the news that they could be in Bari very soon. Sgt. Baker was particularly excited. He nearly forgot the ailments he'd been suffering with. "We're gonna to make it, we're gonna to make!" he said to Sgt. LeClair. "I think you're right Earl!" Sgt. LeClair replied. The relieved crews spent the next couple of days in Split and took things relatively easy. Vis was about thirty-five miles or about three to four hours from Split by boat. The base was operated by the Royal Air Force and the Yugoslavian (Partisan) Air Force as well as US Army Air Corp. It was the only Yugoslavian territory never occupied by the German army. However it was occupied by the Italians in 1941 until the Italians changed sides to the allies in September of 1943 and abandoned the island. Shortly after, the Partisans took control of it. Tito himself used the island as his headquarters for a while after a German commando team nearly captured him at the town of Drvar in present day Bosnia in May of 1944. At this time the airfield was built. The Partisans then shared it with the British and small group of American servicemen. Allied bombers used the island as an emergency landing strip. American Army Air Force personnel of the 15th Air Force made up of mechanics and ground crews were stationed there to repair any bombers that were too damaged to make it back across the Adriatic to Italy. Headed by Captain S.R. Keator who was a hands-on type of officer, Captain Keator was only interested in repairing stricken bombers who landed on the island and getting them back in the air. He never typed a single report. He used to say "If I had a typewriter I'd have to type reports, and if I wrote reports I'd have to file them. We'd rather fix airplanes." Which is what he did, and he ran his outfit well according to those who served under him. The British Royal Air Force based two squadrons of Spitfire fighter planes on the island to support the Partisans. Partisan pilots trained by British pilots also flew Spitfires with the markings of the Yugoslavian Air Force, which was a red star surrounded by a blue circle on their planes. There was also an armed garrison of Partisans soldiers and a few British Army anti-aircraft and coastal gun crews serving as a defense of the island.

By March of 1945, the island and its airstrip were mostly being used for airdrops of supplies to the mainland Partisan units, allied mission outposts. The airfield was also used for evacuating allied air crews, some severely wounded to the Army hospital in Bari. Others like Italian military adversaries and Italian civilians who lived along the Dalmatian coast which had been annexed to Italy before the war were also evacuated from the island. Italians numbering approximately one hundred and fifty thousand were forced to return to Italy after being kicked out of Yugoslavia by the Partisans. Only because Italy abandoned fascism and joined the

Allies were most Italians allowed to return to Italy with little more than their clothes on their backs. But as many as fifteen thousand Italians in Yugoslavia were executed by the Partisans seeking revenge against the former fascist occupiers. Many of the Italian refugees who escaped Yugoslavia by way of Vis, were to be transported by ship back to Italy rather than by air.

The crew by now had various stages of facial growth. They began to resemble the Chetnik soldiers who picked them up back in January. Some of the men had used their army issued knives to trim their whiskers at times but were not too successful at getting as close a shave as they could get from a razor. Lt. Grossman by now had the fullest beard of the crew. Lt. Daniels remarked that he resembled a ship's sea captain much to the chagrin of Lt. Grossman. With the thoughts of arriving back at their base the crew had good reason to joke and laugh about with one another. They would soon be completely in Allied hands.

On Sunday morning, March 25th, the men boarded a forty foot fishing boat manned by an older looking Croatian accompanied by a few Partisan soldiers and young British liaison officer. As soon as all were aboard, the motor on the boat came to life, and a couple of Partisans untied the boat lines from the dock, and the boat turned away from the dock and headed out into the Adriatic. The sea was not too rough sailing between a few other islands a couple of miles off the coast. But once they passed the island of Solta, the white capped waves picked up and the boat rocked a bit more. The Germans had mined much of the waters surrounding the coastal islands, so the pilot of the boat was careful navigating through the waterway making sure to avoid areas the British Royal Navy had charted as dangerous. The boat loaded with the two American bomber crews arrived at the Port of Vis at about one thirty in the afternoon. The British officer led the crews off the boat once they docked. As they disembarked the boat, they noticed a couple of German naval vessels docked in the harbor. These were ships that had been captured by Royal Canadian Navy torpedo boats commanded by Captain Thomas Fuller from Ottawa, Ontario. Captain Fuller carried out several raids and captured several German supply ships in the Adriatic to provide supplies for Tito's Partisans. Captain Fuller was known as the Pirate of the Adriatic.

The crew of Lt. Grossman and Estes were ushered into huts and there they waited for a transport plane to arrive and take them back to Bari. The men were hoping to be evacuated by a C-47 transport plane shortly after arriving. But after two days on the island no airplanes for evacuation were available due to bad weather. With the weather not letting up the British officer told the crew they could travel by one of the captured German supply ships that was docked in the harbor. They would board and sail back to Bari the next day. Lt. Grossman gathered the crew and informed the crew that they could leave by ship as early as tomorrow and be in Bari by sunset that day. The news was greeted with unanimous approval. The crew just wanted to get back to Italy any way possible at this point.

Meanwhile back in the U.S. the families of the crew were still hoping and praying they would hear something more about their missing loved ones. Unbeknownst to the crew, the British officer in Split had sent a message shortly after the crew's arrival at the 15th Air Force headquarters at Bari. The message included a list of names he gathered from the downed air crews that were going to be transported to Vis. The message was forwarded the U.S. Army 26th General Hospital located in Bari as was standard procedure. The message with the names of recovered airmen was sent to prepare the medical staff for new MIA arrivals who must be examined immediately after repatriation before officially clearing them to report for duty. The list of names was shared with the American Red Cross assigned to the hospital. Once the men were cleared by the Army medical staff to return to duty the 15th Air Force would then send an official letter to London for processing the notification of each crewman's return to duty to the office of the Adjutant General office in Washington D.C. From there the Western Union telegrams would be sent to each of the crew's family. The whole process of notifying the next of kin that their loved one was safe and returned to duty would take time, perhaps several days from the time the airmen arrived at Bari until the telegrams reached their homes in the US.

Fortunately for one of the crew, a woman named Beryl Walter was working for the American Red Cross in Bari and just happened to know Lt. Daniels and his family. Miss Walter grew up in Daniel's neighborhood of New Rochelle, NY and was good friends with Lt. Daniel's sister Edith. After joining the Red Cross, she was sent overseas and eventually ended up in Italy attached to the 26th General Hospital. She, in fact, had made trips from Bari to several 15th Air Force bases including the 483rd's at Sterparone where she and other Red Cross members would serve donuts and coffee to airmen who had just returned from missions. When learning that Lt. Daniels was missing in action since late January she had always kept an eye out for any notice of returning MIA's the Red Cross received through the post at the hospital. So when the list of the returning American airmen came to her attention she couldn't believe it. Lt. George Daniels Jr. of New Rochelle, NY was indeed on the list of returning MIA's. She immediately wrote a letter and had it sent to Lt. Daniel's mother Isabelle in New Rochelle via U.S. Army air mail letting her know that by the time she would read the letter, her son would be back in Italy.

At 6:30 the morning of March 28th, the crew were awakened by a British Sargent. "We have a ship leaving port this morning at 09:00 Lieutenant," he said to Lt. Grossman. "You'll be in Bari by days end sir" he continued."That sounds fine Sargent" responded Lt. Grossman. Bari was about one hundred and forty miles away, but to the crew it seemed like twenty. Moving at about fifteen knots and barring any mishap at sea the American crews could expect to arrive in Bari in just under ten hours.

The crews arrived at the ship about thirty minutes before departure and noticed what appeared to be a few hundred Italian civilians boarding ahead of them. Most of them men, but a few women and children as well. The young Italian who joined the crew at Mr. Cvijanovic's farm a few weeks earlier became very excited to finally be among his countrymen who like himself, felt the shame for falling into the trap, whether by force or not, of fascism. As the people crowded aboard the captured ship, the ex-Italian soldier disappeared into a large group of fellow returning countrymen. That was the last the crew saw of him. Once the ship pulled out of the port the ship steamed out into the Adriatic Sea. After about an hour the sea became fairly rough. With dark clouds above and gusty winds, the Adriatic looked grayer than the brilliant blue it looked like at several thousand feet during clear weather missions. Lt. Escardo and Sargents Baker and Taxel, who had already felt sick to their stomachs did their best not to succumb to seasickness. The fact that the crew was used to being bounced around at thirty thousand feet in a B-17 certainly helped keep them from leaning their heads over the side. That and staying top side in the fresh sea air was much better than being crammed below decks where most of the civilians were. For most of the trip the crew seemed subdued. The excitement of getting back to Italy was still evident but after about four hours of steaming along through the choppy sea, many in the crew just settled in quiet thought. Possibly thinking about what they'd all been through the past two and a half months as MIA's. Sgt. Taxel kept thinking of Mr. Cvijanovic and his family. He mentioned to Sgt White about how he would make good on his promise to help the old man's younger sons come to live in America one day.

*Chapter 17*

With every passing hour the crew was getting closer to the reaching the familiar surroundings of the 15$^{th}$ Air Force headquarters at Bari. As the sun was setting in the west during the final half hour of the journey, Sgt. LeClair started scanning the horizon towards the southwest. Suddenly his eyes grew wide and a big smile crossed his face. "Hey! I think I can see the coast of Italy!" he said with cheerful optimism.

"That's Italy alright" replied Sgt. Sparks. The crews of Lieutenants Grossman and Estes were all scanning the coastline trying to locate Bari's port entrance. The closer the ship approached the Italian coast the more the twilight took effect. "I can see Bari!" exclaimed Lt. Daniels. "Are you sure Sandy?" said Lt. Keane. "Yeah I can see the entrance of the harbor!" responded Lt. Daniels. The crew became jubilant at the sight of the city. Sgt. Gourley became quietly emotional as tears of joy streamed down his cheeks as he peered at the harbor a mere four miles in the distance. As he glanced back at his fellow crewmen, many had tears in their eyes.

After the crew settled down a bit, Lt. Grossman was conferring with his officers Lieutenants Escardo, Keane, and Daniels while the rest of the crew was on the forward deck mingling with each other trying to see if they could spot any other ships towards the opening of the harbor. "Ok, well it looks like we'll be back at headquarters soon and I imagine we are going to be interrogated by the brass sooner than later." Lt. Grossman continued. "So listen up. I think it's best we make no mention of Mr. Cvijanovic and his family in our debriefing. I believe it could do more harm to him than good. If any of us mentions the aid we received from the old man and his family by name and our reports somehow leak to the Partisan side, it could lead to trouble for Mr. Cvijanovic since his people are in conflict with the Partisans. And another thing, I'd rather not mention that we split up into two groups in our search for the Partisans. We were only separated for a day anyway." "Why should we not mention it?' asked Lt. Escardo. "Because the Air Force brass are always briefing us that if we are downed in enemy territory, unless we are scattered miles apart during a bailout, it's best for crews to stick together at all times if possible. And I normally believe that too. Well, we did split up and fortunately everything worked out A-OK. But if we report that we split up into two groups even if for only a day, I'm afraid it'll add up to more questions and Army red tape than we'd care to have to go through. As things turned out I'm not sure splitting up was really necessary. All the same the important thing to remember is that we all stayed together the whole time and did not mention any names of those who aided us in evading capture." "Well, how do we explain our evading the Germans for sixty-seven days?" asked Lt. Daniels. "We'll just report that we evaded the enemy for several days before eventually making contact with Yugoslavian Partisans who helped get us to the Adriatic coast," replied Lt. Grossman. "Just keep your personal opinions regarding the Chetniks or Partisans to yourselves, at least for now. If the Army brass were to find out about that Chetnik who took a shot at us, then it might compromise the safety our MIA boys who are still evading capture while in the care of the Chetniks. The Chetniks who tried to get us out already think we abandoned them. If they learn that the brass is officially ending aid because of an incident, they might turn any MIA's in their care over to the Germans or Ustachi out of spite. And who knows what the ememy might do to our boys, especially if their army is in retreat. Because the Germans sure as hell won't take prisoners with them and niether will the Ustachi." Lt. Daniels answered, "As Navigator I'll be required to give our coordinates and the longitude, latitude of the crash site, which I noted right after we crash landed. Won't our location indicate that we were in Chetnik territory?" asked Lt. Daniels. "Not necessarily Sandy. The Chetnik and the Partisan line have been fairly blurred ever since we landed there," responded Lt. Grossman. "So for now just the basic facts like time, place and our overall condition. The less regarding details we put in our report, the sooner we get stateside. Once this wars' over, say whatever you want about our time as MIA's. Look, I don't outrank you guys, so this is NOT an order. Just keep it under advisement.  Now, are we all clear about this?" "Don't worry Bob, as far as I'm concerned, we all just walked to the coast and sailed back to Bari" replied Lt. Keane. "Thanks Tom, now let's inform the rest of the crew," said Lt. Grossman. After informing the enlisted crew, Lt. Grossman was pleased to hear that they all agreed with his advice, though at first Sgt. Taxel was concerned that Mr. Cvjanovic would not receive the credit he was due for all the help he provided to the crew if he were left out of any official report. But Lt. Grossman reassured him by saying he wasn't trying to deny credit or gratitude to the Cvijanovic's, but was in effect trying to protect the family during a time of world war and civil war. But at the same time Lt. Grossman was hoping to avoid a long and tedious interrogation upon he and his crew's eventual return home. He expressed again that once they all returned home and were discharged, everyone including Sgt. Taxel was free to express his feelings about the Cvijanovics to anyone including any military officials. But for now having everybody on the same page regarding the report of their time as MIAs was key to making their repatriation process move quickly and less troublesome. And after all they had been through, the sooner they could get back home to the states the better.

The ship lowered its speed as it approached the entrance to the harbor at Bari as darkness fell on the town. The crew was tired from the long trip across the Adriatic but quite relieved that their MIA ordeal was over at last.

The ship docked in Bari's harbor, and the bomber crews disembarked the ship along with the Italian civilians and a few soldiers. The crew was met by Army personnel and loaded on trucks and taken to the Army 26th General hospital. After arriving at the Army hospital Lt. Estes and his crew were deemed fit for duty in a relatively short period and arrangements were made to return them to their 98th Bomb Group. However Lt. Grossman and crew including Sgt. Whetstone and Cpl. Howe were immediately sent for delousing, much to their relief. They also had all of their clothing boiled. The crewmen were given physical examinations with extra care given to Lt. Escardo who had a harder time adjusting to a regular diet he had consumed after reaching Split. Then they were given a bunk to bed down on with CLEAN white sheets! Some girls from the Red Cross visited the crew, but were not visited by Lt. Daniels' sister Edith's friend Beryl Walter. After posting her letter to Lt. Daniels' mother, she had gone on to a rest camp for a couple of days as part of her Red Cross duties to greet other US airmen sent on R&R.

The next morning of March 29th, the crew was met by an officer of the 15th Air Force headquarters for a brief interrogation about what happened during their mission. Though all of the crew cooperated with the questioning, they kept their answers as short as possible as agreed on the ship the day before. The rest of the day was spent relaxing and enjoying being in the company of the Red Cross servicewomen. Most of the crew were feeling a little better after getting proper nourishment administered by one of the three dietitians on the hospital's medical staff. All of the crew were still suffering from stomach issues. All of them did their best to downplay their ailments, convincing the doctors they were feeling fine so that they could get back to their base sooner rather than later. Whether the Army doctors were convinced that the crew were fit for duty or not, there were more serious patients to care for so they took them for their word. All of them except for Lt. Escardo. He was complaining of feeling worse and was ordered to stay until his stomach "bug" was cured. Aside from a physical examination, the crew also had a psychological exam as well. An Army doctor from the 483rd Office of the Surgeon officially stated in his report to the crew's commanding officer that they all suffered various degrees of stress. One diagnosis in his report stated "Exhaustion from over exertion resulting in combat fatigue suffered since March 28th,1945 and may be regarded as having incurred an injury as a result of an aviation accident within the meaning of Executive Order No. 9195." It is not known why the date was noted as March 28th since the date of the crash was January 21st. Most likely the typist mistakenly put down the same date the examination took place the day before. With this medical report the crew was temporarily relieved of combat flying. It meant they would still collect their full flight pay despite not being scheduled to fly any missions. So instead of taking up valuable space at the Army hospital, which was full of battle-injured fliers, allied soldiers, and Partisans wounded in ground and air combat throughout parts of the Mediterranean theater, they would be officially allowed to continue recuperation at Sterparone. The medical report also recommended that the crew would do well if they would take time for R&R before resuming any assigned duty or transfer from the 483rd. The crew would return to their base with a prescription of taking it easy for a week or two before receiving any transfer orders.

On the afternoon of March 30th Lt. Grossman and crew dropped in and said their goodbyes and well wishes to Lt. Escardo for what would be the last time the rest of the crew would see him. They then left the 26th General Hospital and were taken to the airfield at Bari and flew back to the 483rd bomb group. They flew the approximately eighty miles on a C-47 transport plane back to Sterparone airfield in about twenty-five minutes. Sgt..Whetstone and Cpl. Howe returned to the 484th Bomb Group at Torretto airfield. When the crew arrived at their old base, some of the men like Sgt. Gourley were practically overwhelmed as they touched down on the old familiar runway. It was as if they had finally completed the mission to Vienna. After the crew got off the plane, they noticed all new faces moving about the base. It then dawned on them that most of the other crews from the group they had flown missions with had already finished their tour and were sent home or were subsequently shot down and listed as killed in action, POW's or missing. Lieutenants Grossman, Keane and Daniels were set up in officers quarters while

Sargents LeClair, Gourley, Sparks, Taxel, Baker and White were sent over to the enlisted huts. First order of business was for the crew to be given an extra change of clothes and given rations. Not long after landing at their base a Red Cross "club mobile" truck arrived to serve coffee and donuts. Lt. Daniels decided to join in line for a donut and cup of coffee. Suddenly the Red Cross woman setting out the trays of donuts noticed Lt. Daniels in line and called out,"Hey Sandy!" It was Beryl Walter. Lt. Daniels was a bit embarrassed being called by his nickname in front of a bunch of servicemen, most of whom were new arrivals that he hadn't been acquainted with at all.

He jogged over to Beryl and greeted her. "Well, Hi, Beryl! What are you doing here?" asked Lt. Daniels. "I'm stationed at Bari with the Red……uh, never mind about me, what about you? I was worried sick when your sister told me you were listed as missing in action, but then I found out you were safe when your name was posted on a list we received from the Army hospital," she replied. "I'm O.K., Beryl. Just tired, but happy to be back." Lt. Daniels said reassuringly.

"I wrote your mother when I found out you were coming back to Bari," said Miss Walter. "Thanks, Beryl! We just arrived today from Bari. As soon as we are allowed, I'm going to see about sending my Mom and Dad a telegram. I'm sure the War Department has already sent one, but I'd like to tell the folks I'm ok personally" said Lt. Daniels. Miss Walter was by now getting summoned to return to her duties as more men were lining up to the Red Cross truck. "Well I have to get back to work Sandy. So nice to see you! I'll write another letter to your Mom today when I get back to Bari. See you back in New Rochelle!" she said as she disappeared into the surging line of servicemen. "Goodbye Beryl. Take care of yourself!" replied Lt. Daniels. The short visit from a family friend back home left Lt. Daniels walking back to his quarters with a good feeling inside. The war was winding down in Europe, and he knew he'd be coming home soon.

After a while, each of the men was visited by a Captain Mullins for more interrogation. Captain Mullins also informed the crew that they all had enough points to return to the States. They were through with flying combat missions for the 483rd and could enjoy their R&R until transfer orders to the States would come through, though for most of the crew, receiving their official discharge wouldn't take place for a few months. But spending their remaining months on active duty stateside was just fine with them.

For Lt. Grossman and the rest of the crew, being grounded from flying combat missions, though expected, was great news.  The crew could volunteer for assignment to a bomb group in the Pacific theater if anyone wished to. But they would have to be re-evaluated and deemed fit for combat duty. All of the crew were credited with flying over forty combat bombing missions.

Back in New Rochelle, upon receiving the letter Miss Walter had written when she first learned Lt. Daniels and his fellow crewmen were safe and about to sail out of Split, Mrs. Daniels immediately wrote a letter to Lt. Grossman's wife, Madeline. She then spread the news of the crew's safe return from Yugoslavia by letter to the mother of Earl Baker. But that is as far as the passing of the message went for reasons unknown. But at least the families of Lt. Grossman, Lt. Daniels and Sgt. Baker had finally received some good news. Though in a few days time word of the crews returning safely to their base would reach all of the crew's family by way of the Western Union telegrams.

## Chapter 18

On April 3$^{rd}$ the crew went into town to get their hair trimmed and their more than seventy days of facial hair shaved, though a few like Lt. Keane kept the mustache he had grown shortly after arriving in Italy. The Italian barber at first did not want to shave Lt. Grossman's beard. He thought it was too nice to shave. But eventually he caved in and gave Lt. Grossman a nice clean shave. The crew had reason to spruce up. The next day they were ordered to show up in dress formation and receive their Air Medals. The morning of the small ceremony the crew lined up and were greeted by Lt. Colonel Willard Sperry who was acting group commander while the regular group commander Col. Paul Barton was away on other duties. One by one Lt.Col. Sperry read off the crew's name commending each them for a job well done for our grateful nation. As they heard their name called, each man stepped forward and Col. Sperry pinned the medals above the left pocket on their dress uniforms and gave them each a return salute and hardy handshake and then exchanged a salute. The whole ceremony lasted about ten minutes. After the crewmen returned to their respective huts they received orders to report to the air base at Naples. From there they would wait for transfer orders to the States. The next available flight to Naples was a couple of days away. They would fly to Naples and sit tight until the transfer orders were complete.

On April 7$^{th}$ the crew boarded a B-17 and took off from Sterparone Air Field for the last time. The bomber had been converted for use as transport for crews and high ranking officers to shuttle them to and from the many Army Air Force bases in southern Italy. After arriving in Naples the crew reported on base and were quartered at the airfield that was used by the Twelfth Air Force and more recently by the Air Transport Command. The ATC was responsible for transporting military equipment and supplies to the various combat squadrons in the Mediterranean Theater as well as all the other theaters of operation throughout the world during the war. It was also used to transport personal military back to the United States. Many of the crew had been to Naples before as it was the port to catch the boat to Capri where they spent most of their R&R. But this time the crew opted to spend their off duty time stay sightseeing and visiting a few watering holes. By now they were in great spirits while getting a chance to blow off steam after their experience as MIAs.  Everyone in the crew was feeling better physically except Sgt. Baker, who was nursing his sore feet and still feeling generally in a run down condition. He spent the majority of the time on base recuperating. Some of the crew such as Lt. Daniels and Sgt. Taxel began to think in retrospect, marveling how very lucky they were to have avoided capture or even to have survived their time in Yugoslavia, while other members of the crew, including Lieutenants Grossman, Keane and Sgt. LeClair kept their thoughts on what the future held for them as civilians back home.

Sgt. Gourley couldn't wait to see his mother again. He was worried about the telegrams letting loved ones know that their boys were safe would take forever reaching his small town in the southeast corner of Colorado.

On the evening of April 12th the crew received the tragic news that President Roosevelt had died of a massive cerebral hemorrhage in Warm Springs, GA. After the initial shock of the news, (the President had kept hidden the fact that he was in ill health since he won re-election in late 1944) a more somber mood took hold of the US servicemen in Naples throughout the air base. Whether Americans were for or against FDR's domestic policies, he was still a revered leader of the Western Allies and held in the highest regard by a vast majority of the free world. His homeland approval rating had peaked to a whopping 83% in early days after Pearl Harbor. With his death, Harry S. Truman was sworn in as President of the United States. Truman had only been Vice-President since January 20th,1945 and rarely even saw FDR during his brief stint as his second in command. In fact Roosevelt never briefed Truman on the Atomic bomb or the unfolding problems with Soviet Russia. Suddenly the country looked to Truman to solve all of its wartime problems. After being sworn in, Truman told reporters when asked how it felt to be President, that it felt like the moon, the stars and all of the planets had fallen on him.

The day after Roosevelt's death, on April 13th the crew received their transfer orders to report to bases in the States. Each of the crew was ordered to report to air bases as near as possible to their hometowns as a "courtesy" of the Army Air Force. It would also save Uncle Sam on homeward-bound travel cost once the men were discharged from the service. The enlisted men of the crew, Sargents Gourley and White were ordered to report to Ft. Logan, Colorado. Sgt. Sparks was to report to Camp Atterbury, Indiana, Sgt.s Taxel and Baker to Ft. Dix, New Jersey, and Sgt. LeClair to Ft. Devens, Mass. As for the officers, Lt. Grossman and Lt. Daniels were ordered to report to Ft. Dix and Lt. Keane to Ft. Devens. Lt. Escardo, who was still recuperating from a bad case of dysentery stayed in Italy for the time being. Before having to report for duty at their designated bases stateside, the men were given a thirty day furlough to begin soon after their arrival on U.S. soil. All of the crew would eventually be honorably discharged from military service before or a few weeks after the war in the Pacific drew to a close.

Naples would be the last place the officers and the enlisted men of the crew would all be together as servicemen. On April 15th Lieutenants Grossman, Daniels and Keane flew out of Naples on a C-47 transport plane bound for Oran, Algeria for a brief stop before arriving at the airfield at Casablanca, Morocco. The next day on April 16th, Sargents LeClair, Gourley, White, Sparks, Taxel, and Baker caught transport following the same route. After spending a few days in Casablanca with the officers quartered in a local hotel and the enlisted crew staying on the base, the crew waited for transport back to the States. The air base at Casablanca was used as a staging area for all American aircraft for the European Theater of Operations during the war. The Moroccan city was the site of the Casablanca conference attended by President Roosevelt and Prime Minister Churchill in 1943 when the two allied leaders discussed the war's progress. But the crew saw nothing that resembled the Casablanca made famous by the Humphrey Bogart film. They instead stayed close to their quarters during their stay after being warned by other servicemen of the perils of the city. Outside of the hotel area and/or the air base, the city was one filled with poor sanitation and extreme poverty among impoverished men, women, and children begging in the streets all day. Most members of the armed forces were advised not to leave the designated safe zone of the city. It could be dangerous for American service personnel to venture out into the city without an armed MP close by. A simple wrong turn down the wrong alley could lead to an unsuspecting young American soldier or airmen getting his throat cut for his wristwatch by Moroccan thieves. A strict curfew was enforced by the American MP's beginning at each sundown.

By mid to late April with the war in Europe only a few weeks from its conclusion, the Air Transport Command were making daily flights with full loads of servicemen. Mostly trips were made by air crews who finished their mission requirement and were returning to the U.S. and also wounded soldiers and airmen who were well enough to make the long flight across the Atlantic. So with many servicemen signed up for flights for the next few days, the crew would have to wait their turn on the next available flight. Finally on the morning April 20th the three officers, Lieutenants Grossman, Daniels and Keane boarded another plane, this time the larger C-54 transport and took off in short order. The flight plan included fuel stops in the Azores and Newfoundland before finally arriving at Washington D.C.'s National Army Air Base late that evening. The enlisted portion of the crew, Sargents LeClair, Gourley, White, Sparks, Taxel and Baker flew out of Casablanca on another C-54 early the next morning and arrived in Washington the evening of April 22nd. So happy to be on U.S. soil at last after a very long flight, a bleary-eyed Sgt. Gourley kissed the ground after disembarking the plane.

Upon the crew's arrival in Washington the officers and enlisted men were kept separated and each was told to report to the base headquarters for more interrogation. All of the crew was interrogated individually by high ranking Army intelligence officers.

These interrogations were more intense than the ones they had gone through back in Italy. The crew was asked for names, places, specific escape routes, underground contacts, the cause of crash landing, how exactly did they evade the enemy, why couldn't they reach friendly airfields in Hungary. Lt. Grossman endured the more rigorous of the interrogations. As first pilot and leader, he was considered the most responsible for the well being of the crew. He was asked several questions about the mission. Questions for example, where and when they lost sight of the formation? Where did they crash? All of which he answered as accurately as he recollected.

Lt. Daniels even gave the intelligence officers the exact longitude/latitude on where the plane crashed. Lt. Keane gave the questioning officers the map he had drawn of their routes taken in Yugoslavia. Though he'd wanted to keep the map, it was now the property of the U.S. Government and that's the last he ever saw of it. One intelligence officer in particular, an army Major, suggested during Sgt. Gourley's turn in the questioning that the crew should pay Uncle Sam for the B-17 lost in the crash. Fortunately a Colonel rebuked him for making such a ridiculous suggestion and the Major was asked to leave the room. With the war in Europe still going on the crew still stuck to their plan. Not one crew member was said to have mentioned any names of the Chetniks, Partisans or the Cvijanovic family. Each man only mentioned them by group association. The Chetniks were the Chetniks and the Partisans were the Partisans. Sgt. LeClair did mention the fact that everyone was still experiencing stomach problems and how they all (except Lt. Escardo) downplayed that fact to the doctors in Italy so they could get home sooner. Other than that, the information about their time spent as MIAs was as short and brief as possible. (Note: A few months later Lieutenants Grossman, Keane and Daniels were asked to fill out a questionnaire regarding the condition of each enlisted man of the crew from the time the plane went down until they were last seen in Italy.)

After the interrogations in Washington finished, the crew returned to their temporary quarters while their thirty-day furlough orders were prepared. Also transportation by way of train needed to be arranged to send each man to his hometown. In the meantime each crew member was allowed to send Western Union telegrams letting the loved ones that they had made it to Washington and would be home on furlough in a few days. Though some of the crew were able to send cablegrams to their families from Naples, the telegrams from U.S. soil had a stronger impact. To the families of the crew, it meant that their boys were no longer in harm's way. Each of the crew would arrive at their hometowns by early May to begin their furloughs. By that time Adolf Hitler would be dead in Berlin. What remained of the German Armed forces was in shambles.

*Chapter 19*

As the crew met their homecomings, the reunions with loved ones were no doubt quite emotional. Lt. Grossman finally returned to New York and rushed into the embrace of his wife Madeline after nearly a year away from home. The same emotional greetings would be experienced by the other married crew members Sargents Baker, Taxel and White with their wives. And all of the crew were to be given a heartfelt welcome home from by their mothers, fathers and other family members who never gave up hope no matter how long their boys were missing in action. Many tears of joy were shed, especially by the mothers upon their son's return home. Local newspapers in each of the hometowns of the crew spread the news that they had returned to duty in Italy on March 30th and were now back in the U.S.

While some of the crew were already home or on their way home to begin their furloughs, the war in Europe officially ended on the 8th of May. VE day was celebrated throughout the Allied nations of the world. But with Japan still in the fight in the Pacific, the celebrations soon died down. A couple of days after VE day, it was the business of war as usual in America.

After the crew members completed their furloughs in late May and early June, each of them boarded trains that would take them to their stateside duty and their final assignment before discharge. Most of the crew stayed in duties related to aviation, but no one in the crew volunteered to join a combat bombing crew in the Pacific Theater. Sgt. Sparks had other plans altogether. He applied and was accepted for training to become an MP (Military Policeman) and eventually made Provost Sergeant. He was in charge of a squad of Army sentries at Fort Thomas, Kentucky.

Back in Italy, Lt. Escardo was by now well enough to be transferred stateside as well. He received orders to transfer to the west coast to the Army Air Force re-distribution base at Santa Monica, California where he would train as pilot for a B-29 crew before shipping out to a base in the Pacific. Having only completed eleven combat missions, he needed more combat missions to finish his tour. With his status as an MIA in the Mediterranean theater and the war in Europe over, his only real option to finish his tour of combat missions would be to join a bombardment crew in the Pacific theater of operations. He arrived at Santa Monica in late May 1945 and was promoted to First Lieutenant. For the next two months, he would continue flight training out of Mines Field at El Segundo, CA at what is today the location of the Los Angeles International Airport. Tragically Lt. Escardo never made it to the Pacific Theater or even to his home Lima, Peru. He was killed on July 31st, 1945 when his plane crashed in the Pacific Ocean five miles offshore from the town of Playa Del Rey, California. Also killed was his twenty-five-year-old co-pilot Lt. Gerald Bauer of Denver, Colorado. Lt. Bauer had also recently returned from flying combat bombing missions over Europe. The two pilots were the only ones on board the training flight that day. Lt. Escardo had recently turned thirty years old. Only a few pieces of wreckage in the water were found by the Coast Guard search plane. The two pilots bodies were never found. The loss of Lt. Escardo no doubt came as quite a shock to his family back home in Lima. After surviving combat flying that he kept from his parents and making it back to the U.S. after nearly seventy days as an MIA, the news of his death was also met with sadness and disappointment by each of the crew when they learned of his death years later.

A week after Lt. Escardo's death, the U.S. dropped the first atomic bomb over the Japanese city of Hiroshima. Three days later on August 9th, a second atomic bomb was successfully detonated over Nagasaki. On August 14th, the Empire of Japan agreed in principle to unconditional surrender. Japan formally surrendered on September 2nd, 1945 in Tokyo Bay and thus ended the greatest human conflict in history. It is believed that eighty million people died during the war. Of those who died, fifty to fifty-five million were civilians including nineteen to possibly as high as twenty-eight million that died due to disease and or starvation.

Lt. Daniels was already honorably discharged from the service and was back home when news of the bombs were dropped. Most of the other crew members were honorably discharged a few days after Japan surrendered.

With their service during the war behind them, the crew now could completely focus on life going forward as civilians. But the transition from an air combat bombing crew to ordinary civilian would take some getting used to. For the most part the crew talked very little about the details of their war experience to family and friends. As with most veterans of the war they believed that any boasting about their exploits during the war would dishonor those comrades who did not return home. They were uncomfortable when being called "heroes," especially soon after returning home. The crew felt that they were just doing their jobs while serving in the Army Air Force. Nothing more, nothing less. As far as they were concerned, the many young men in the 483rd bomb group who were killed in action were the real heroes. Throughout the years after the war, some of the crew would correspond with each other through letters and or Christmas letters. A few of the crew would meet in person on rare occasions through various reunions put on by the 483rd Association in cities like Dayton, Boston, or Kansas City. Only two or three of the MIA crew were able to attend any particular reunion at the same time and place. But the MIA crew were never together as a complete group after leaving Italy in 1945.

In June of 1974, Mr. and Mrs. Cvijanovic came to the U.S. to visit with their sons in upstate New York in the town of Wappingers Falls near Poughkeepsie. Before his parent's visit Momcilo Cvijanovic contacted Stanley Taxel who contacted the 483rd Association in an effort to locate the other members of the crew so they could all be invited to the reunion with the Cvijanovic's at Momcilo's home. The gathering was held on the weekend of June 15th and 16th. Unfortunately only four of the crew were able to attend the gathering. Those attending were Lt. Daniels, and Sargents Taxel, Gourley and White who flew in together from Denver. The Cvijanovic's other son Milo lived nearby in Pleasant Valley and also attended. The local and Associated Press was also informed of the reunion and sent reporters to cover the gathering. Those attending the reunion celebrated well into the night. Though Mr. and Mrs. Cvjanovic couldn't speak a word of English, pure joy was had by all who attended. Daniels, Taxel, White and Gourley hugged and kissed the old couple now in their eighties who were just as overjoyed to see them. With tears streaming down his cheeks Mr. Cvijanovic exclaimed in his native Serbian language what translated to, "They still seem like they're my sons!" Many toasts were lifted with cups filled with rakija, the same drink Mr. Cvijanovic gave the airmen when they stayed at his farm during the war. Later they cooked a pig and a lamb in an open pit as was the custom in Yugoslavia for important celebrations while traditional Yugoslavian polka music played throughout the day. As James Gourley later said, "It was one hell of a party!"

A reporter from the Associated Press and a local reporter from the Poughkeepsie Journal along with a staff photographer were in attendance to cover the gathering.

The reunion was featured in several newspapers coast to coast. During the evening as the group was settling down to enjoy their dinner Mr. Cvijanovic, with his son Momcilo acting as translator, told the crew about what happened to him shortly after the war ended. He told the crew that Tito's Communists took control over parts of the country after the Germans were defeated, and eventually a neighbor informed the police that the Cvjanovic's harbored an American aircrew. With that information Mr. Cvjanovic was arrested and taken into custody. He was then severely beaten while his wife and children were forced to watch. Had he not been as well known in the community, he most certainly would have been considered a traitor and would have been shot. He was eventually released from custody, but his legs were struck so many times during the beating that he eventually had to have his left leg amputated due to damaged blood vessels. He had to use a prosthetic leg and a cane to walk.

After the reunion at Momcilo's home the elder Cvijanovic's returned to Yugoslavia a few days later. It was their only trip to America but one they would never forget.The crew members who did not attend the gathering at Momcilo's home had various reasons for being absent. Some had prior commitments that weekend. Others were traveling on family vacations. One crew member (Sgt. Baker) was too ill to make the trip up from Baltimore. Sgt. Sparks was particularly upset that he missed the reunion due to work obligations in Cincinnati. He later said that he should have just taken time off and flown out to New York to be with his war time comrades and the family that sheltered him during the war.

One must remember that this gathering was held in the nineteen-seventies. At the time the crew was in their early fifties with established employment careers and family responsibilities. For Lieutenants Grossman and Keane and Sgt. LeClair, the war, though twenty-nine years in the past, was still fresh in their minds. It's quite possible they simply just weren't ready to relive memories specifically from a very turbulent time in their lives. One thing is known for sure and that is that each of the crew never forgot their ordeal as MIAs in Yugoslavia in 1945. More importantly one can only hope that those who hear of their experience all those years ago never forget their sacrifice.

## *Epilogue*

After his honorable discharge from the Army Air Force, Lt. Robert Grossman returned to New York and to his wife, Madeline. Robert would work in the jewelry business. He and Madeline would later raise two daughters in upstate New York before retiring and moving to Florida. Robert passed away in the summer of 2007.

After his death in the plane crash in 1945, Lt. Carlos Escardo's remains were never found. It is unknown if there is a memorial site in his native Peru.

Lt. Thomas Keane Jr. returned home to Dorchester, Massachusetts. He worked for the Massachusetts Transit Authority (MTA) in Boston. Thomas married his sweetheart Mary Hogan who grew up a few blocks from his home. The Keane's would go on to raise two daughters. Thomas passed away in the fall of 1991.

Lt. George Daniels Jr. returned to New Rochelle, New York. He soon began dating and later marrying Dorothy Fisher. George worked in sales for a sign manufacturer in New York City. They would raise two sons and three daughters. After living in Mt. Vernon, New York for a while, they eventually would settle in Stamford, Connecticut. George passed away in 1987.

Tech Sgt. Robert LeClair returned to Keene, New Hampshire. Robert worked as a machinist and built homes occasionally on weekends. He married Jane and had four children, two sons, and two daughters. Years later he and Jane divorced, and Robert remarried a woman named Glenna. He and Glenna had no children together. Robert passed away in 1999.

Tech Sgt. Stanley Taxel returned to Brooklyn, New York and to his wife Elaine. He worked in the stationery business and also continued his passion for photography. Stanley and Elaine would become the parents of two sons. The Taxel's also divorced after more than twenty years of marriage. Stanley made good on his promise to Dragutin Cvijanivic and eventually traveled to Washington DC and appealed to the Chief of Staff of the 15th Air Force Commander, General Nathan Twining. He successfully secured entry visa's and sponsored two of Mr. Cvijanovic's children, sons Momcilo in 1958 and Milorad in 1966. The Cvijanovic boys lived with the Taxels for a while in New York. He helped Dragutin's sons attain eventual US citizenship. They both went to colleges in the States and earned degrees and went on to successful careers. Stanley made several trips back to Yugoslavia after the war to visit the Cvijanovics and was a strong advocate for the Serbian people during their long-standing conflict with Croatia. He even wrote to President George H.W. Bush to urge support for the Serbs by reminding the President of their assisting downed American fliers and of Serbian families like the Cvijanovics who risked their lives by supplying food and shelter to him and his fellow aircrew during World War II. Stanley passed away in the winter of 1995.

S Sgt..Russell White returned to Colorado to his wife, Wilma. He worked in the insurance business for several years. The couple had two children, a son, and a daughter and made their home in Fort Collins. Russell passed away in 2000.

S Sgt Virgle Sparks returned home to Cincinnati. He worked as an engineer in the power plant at Celotex Corporation. Virgle married Sylvia, and together they had had three children, two sons and a daughter. Virgle passed away in the summer of 2006.

S Sgt. Earl Baker returned home to Baltimore and attended Johns Hopkins University for two years. He and his wife Audrey raised two daughters. Earl worked for the Baltimore Gas and Electric Company. Earl passed away in the summer of 1975.

S Sgt. James Gourley went home to Lycan, Colorado (now known as Two Buttes.) Shortly after returning home in late August of 1945, he met and started dating Mary May Mackey. Less then a year later he and Mary May were married. James purchased some land after the war and he worked as a farmer. The couple would go on the raise five children, four daughters and a son. James continued farming until he retired at the ripe old age of eighty-nine. On June 5, 2016, James and Mary May celebrated their seventieth wedding anniversary. The entire town along with family and friends (totaling of about one hundred people) celebrated the event with them. James and Mary May continue to live happily at their home in Two Buttes, Colorado.

Momcilo Cvijanovic lives in Manassas, Virginia. He was married and raised a son and a daughter in upstate New York before moving to Virginia after divorcing his wife several years ago. Momcilo (Mo) lives a very active life in retirement. He enjoys traveling and participating in several charitable activities that involve his local church. He exercises regularly by swimming, jogging, and occasionally hiking, even at the age of eighty-two. He visits Sgt. Gourley in Colorado on special occasions. He is the last surviving member of the Cvijanovic family.

And thus brings to a conclusion a remarkable story of a group of young ordinary men brought together by a world at war, and like hundreds of thousands of other young Americans airmen of the Army Air Force serving in Europe during World War Two, they were asked to perform what people would call extraordinary acts of bravery. While many American air crews were listed as missing in action and returned to active duty with the help of friendly citizens or soldiers who supported the allies, this particular crew survived a crash landing behind enemy lines and in a country that was in the midst of several ethnic struggles resulting in thousands of deaths. Despite the odds being against them, this bomber crew was able to evade capture and a likely execution at the hands of either the Ustachis or Nazis for well over two months. But without the bravery of Dragutin and Vasilia Cvijanovic the crew may never have made it back to Italy alive. They put their entire family at risk by giving what little food they had and shelter to the crew for over fifty days at their farm. The crew was also fortunate to have made contact with the Chetnik soldiers, especially those who first picked them up after the crash. Though some of their Chetnik escorts later showed contempt towards the Americans and others were more threatening, as a group they stuck their necks out for the allied airmen. And regardless of their inability to get the crew out of Yugoslavia despite several promises to do so, the Chetniks nonetheless provided the crew the much needed protection from the Germans and Ustachis while leading them to and from their outposts and the Cvijanovic farm. It should also be noted that the Partisans soldiers, who were successful in escorting the crew to the Adriatic coast, were given much thanks and gratitude by each of the crew.

As the years pass and surviving veterans of World War Two are becoming less in numbers, it is we as people of a peaceful and free society who must never forget the incredible sacrifice made by those who fought and died in the greatest conflict in human history. Without their sacrifice, the landscape of the free world might look vastly different, even by today's standards. And with the help and cooperation from families like the Cvjanovics during the war, many veterans were able to survive their ordeals and return home and live out their lives in peace and prosperity.

From this author to the crew of B-17 #44-6423: officers Lt. Grossman, Lt. Escardo, Lt. Keane, Lt. Daniels, and enlisted men T Sgt. LeClair, T Sgt. Taxel, S Sgt. Baker, S Sgt. Sparks, S Sgt. White and S Sgt. Gourley and to non-crew members S Sgt. Larry Whetsone and Cpl. Robert Howe, you served our nation with honor and with pride for your country. Your courage and dedication never to be be forgotten. Thank you for a job well done! And last but not least, much gratitude and thanks must be given to Dragutin and Vasilia Cvijanovic and their family. The crew would not have survived without your act of heroism.

## "She's Not Hard To Handle"

She's not too hard to handle

Yet she can take a lot,

And all our boys sure love her,

For she gives them all she's got,


She certainly is a beauty,

With her body built so strong,

And should you ever take her out,

She'll never treat you wrong,


She's out both early and late,

Regardless of the weather,

And tho she's far from being light

She handles like a feather,


She really is a wonderful thing,

For she does more than her share,

So if she ever feels bad,

Let's give her the best of care,


I see you guys are smiling,

For you are thinking of a dame,

So I'll not keep you in suspense,

I'll tell you all her name,


Some fellows call her "Princess",

Still others call her "Queen",

But on the line she's better known,

As our own "B-17".


THE END

Photo taken of eight members of the crew in mid April 1945 in Italy shortly before departing to the U.S.

Front row left to right: S Sgt Russell White, S Sgt. Virgle Sparks, S Sgt. James Gourley, and T Sgt. Robert LeClair
Standing left to right: S Sgt. Earl Baker, Lt. George Daniels II, Lt. Robert Grossman, and Lt. Thomas Keane

Missing from photo: 2nd Lt. Carlos Escardo and T Sgt. Stanley Taxel who were still recuperating in the hospital.

Pilot Lt. Robert Grossman

Bombardier Lt. Thomas Keane

Co-Pilot 2<sup>nd</sup> Lt. Carlos Escardo
(only known photo, albeit poor
quality)

Navigator, Lt. George Daniels II

Engineer / Top Turret Gunner, T Sgt. Robert LeClair

Waist Gunner, S Sgt. James Gourley
Italy April 1945

Ball Turret Gunner,
S Sgt. Virgle Sparks

Waist Gunner/Armorer
S Sgt. Earl Baker

Tail Gunner,
S Sgt. Russell White

Radioman T Sgt. Stanley Taxel

Lt. Thomas Keane with wife Mary
- Boston 1945

S Sgt. Virgle Sparks dressed
in Chetnik uniform - Yugoslavia 1945

Cvijanovic Family - Yugoslavia 1945
(Dragutin and wife Vasilia back row center)

Lt. Robert Grossman
- Italy 1945

Pin marks the global coordinates on the field in Yugoslavia where the crew's B-17 crash landed on January 21, 1945 - as it looks in Bosnia-Herzegovina 2018.

Reunion with crew members and Cvijanovic family (left to right): T Sgt. Stanley Taxel, Dragutin Cvijanovic, Lt. George Daniels, S Sgt. James Gourley, Vasilia Cvijanovic, Milorad (Milo) Cvijanovic, S Sgt. Russell White, 483rd BG member Clyde Miller and Momchilo (Mo) Cvijanovic in Wappingers Falls, NY, June 1974.

S Sgt. James Gourley at his home in Two Buttes, CO - 2016

Momchilo Cvijanovic at his home in Manassas,VA - 2015.

Made in the USA
Columbia, SC
29 December 2018